T0285514

# STRONGER
## THAN YOUR PAIN

**Overcome Self-Doubt, Anxiety, And Depression
And Become The Master Of Your Destiny.**

## ALEX WASSOM

ISBN: 979-8-35093-840-1
ISBN eBook: 979-8-35093-276-8

Dedicated to my wife, Ashley. When I am not stronger than my pain, you always have strength to give me. For that, I am ever grateful.

To my children. You are my "why" behind all that I do. I pray with all the strength I have that this book and the lessons within can help you endure the struggles life will inevitably throw at you.

To my parents. Thank you for dealing with me during my dark years. Most importantly, thank you for never giving up on me. Thank you for a wonderful foundation that you provided me. I hope I can do for my children what you have done for me.

I love you, all.

/AW/

# CONTENTS

Me during my sick years, slowly fading away at 18.
If only this young man knew what I know now…

# PREFACE

My adolescent years were some of the toughest years of my life, as they are for many of us. I think they were also some of the toughest years for my parents due to what I put them through. Having lived through those years, I've come out the other side with a newfound perspective on life. And I state "having lived through those years" directly, because I almost didn't live through them.

When I was 16, my grandmother, Shirley, died of melanoma. It happened quickly and within intimate proximity to me. It started in her home, which I spent a lot of time in, and ended in my parents' home - in my home. This wasn't the first time I had dealt with death in my life. However, it was the first time it affected me and led me to ask deep questions about life itself. Where did we come from? Why are we here? Where do we go after we die? What is the purpose of life? This was a lot for my 16-year-old brain and heart to question, and even more so to answer and understand.

To avoid telling the intimate parts of the story here, I'll get to the point. The death of my grandmother led to the near death of me. With her passing, I ended up hitting rock bottom and then dug my grave. The only thing that got me out were the tools I share in this book. This is my reason for writing this. In the 16 years that have passed since my grandmother's death, life has happened and I have learned a lot, mostly through repetitious failure. Through my stories, shared studies, hand written notes, and chapter activities, I hope to capture lessons I've learned through those repetitious failures so that you don't have to go through every single one yourself. My goal is to use this book to share the lessons learned and the tools developed to overcome extreme self doubt, anxiety, and depression. For some of us, it's extreme trauma that causes most of our stresses. However, for most, our self-doubt, anxiety, and depression approaches via 1,000 paper cuts.

This is now my passion, dare I say my calling, in life. To help others understand and apply these tools to better their lives and find themselves and their purpose.

While my target audience is young adults, specifically 16-to-28-year-olds, this book is for everyone. I use these tools every day. My friends and their parents use these tools every day. One must apply these tools constantly, since life is an ongoing process of change and development. So regardless of age, background, or experience, these tools are for you.

A special note for parents: please read this, not to push your children, but to understand them. These years are some of the most formative years in their lives and will have a lasting impact. They may be some of the roughest years. But, if approached correctly, can also be some of the most positively memorable years. Use the tools in this book for yourself to gain your own intrapersonal relationship. Lead by example, work hand in hand, and I promise that your relationship with your children will improve.

A special note for young adults: lean on your parents and / or your support network as much as you can. Learn from their mistakes to avoid having to make every mistake on your own. While their method of support may not be how you'd like to receive it, acknowledge that what they're saying holds great value regardless of how they say it. They're only trying to help, and believe me, we can all use some help - so take it.

Here is to the never ending project that is ourselves and our lives. I hope this book can provide you with just one tool you can use to make your project just a little more beautiful and help you become Stronger Than Your Pain. Let's get to work.

/AW/

# FOREWORD

In this age of countless voices vying for attention across all the media platforms available today, Alex Wassom is one of those unique individuals who can captivate, inspire, and ignite something within us. As his father, I will admit to an infinite amount of very positive prejudice toward, and love for Alex today, but at times, as a "villain" of sorts in his book, and as the writer of this Foreword, I also get to acknowledge that it wasn't always easy. In fact, life in the Wassom household was painful, dark and difficult for all of our family members during Alex's upbringing between his ages of 16 and 20. As his parents, Rosanne and I never stopped loving him and supporting him, although at times it seemed that we had absolutely no tools that could help him or ourselves. We could see his anger and desperation building after the death of my mother, and we were often the focus of it. As difficulties often do in many families, these challenges tested our marriage, our faith in ourselves and in each other, and it tested our self-perception as parents and partners. It made us question how the parenting skills that were successful with our other sons were such a failure with Alex. We questioned how such a "golden child," who lit up every room he entered prior to age 16, could so rapidly go from happy, optimistic and engaged in life to suicidal and threatening in such a short period of time. At the time I was taking great pride in helping my mom with her terminal illness, I never anticipated that supporting her during her final days would send our son on a deeply dark and negative spiral, but I think that's how life can be at times -- it can hit you hard from the blindside.

During the past 10 years, Alex has taken a "man on a mission" approach to self-healing on a physical level (dietary and strength training), and on an emotional and psychological level, and has emerged ready to share his journey with young people, parents and families who have a need to hear his message. He is very passionate about his mission, and I am extraordinarily proud to pen the Foreword for his remarkable book as I believe it can bring hope, healing and health to individuals and families experiencing teenage and young adult depression, along with providing tools our family didn't have at that difficult time. Alex has distilled his pain into rational thought, daily discipline, and strong actions, and has developed tools that others - young people and parents alike, can benefit from.

For young people battling depression, loneliness and other challenges in this crazy world, and for parents and other family members struggling to help their children through these difficulties, may you find solutions, solace, inspiration, courage and confidence that strengthens your resolve to make it through the dark clouds that accompany journeys like Alex's. There's a better life on the other side of these dark valleys, and Alex has provided an amazing source of information and inspiration to light the way.

**To Alex....** Thank you for putting in the arduous work you've completed thus far, and for climbing the hills and turning the corners you had to conquer to become the awesome man you are today. Thank you for your part in rehabilitating what is today a beautiful relationship between us. Our connection was always there, but it's stronger and deeper and more enjoyable than ever before, and that would not have happened without your persistence, your commitment to your family and the work you've invested in yourself. Thank you for involving Rosanne and me in your life and in the lives of your beautiful wife and daughters. Painful experiences like we went through can tear generations apart, and we're so thankful that we are a very loved and involved part of your world today. Thank you for asking me to write this Foreword -- I do it with much love, pride and respect for you and your journey! I'm certain your book will help people in many ways.

Love,

Dad

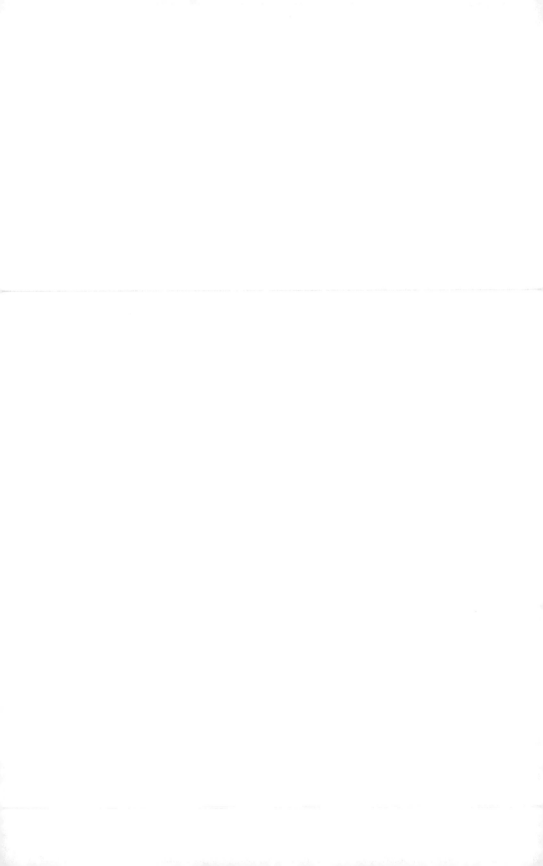

# CHAPTER 0
## SHIRLEY AND THE WOLFE

———————————

There I was, yet again. Standing in my room by myself, contemplating my existence. This time was different, though. The contemplation had expanded beyond thought and into action - into life. The irony was that with the life I was giving to the thoughts was leading to the death of me.

I stared into a mirror I had shattered days, maybe weeks prior. At this point I had lost track of time - same crap, different day mentality. As I stared into the mirror, I realized how well it was doing its job. Its shattered and splintered appearance reflected my shattered and splintered soul. I stared and wondered how much more I was going to take, how much more I could take, how much more hell could I continue to live through.

Like I said, the irony of giving life to my thoughts as action was that the action was to take my life. That action was me testing the boundaries, finding out just how far I could take it and if I could, in fact, do it. Looking into the shattered mirror that so closely resembled the inner workings of what was left of me, I could see my left arm cut, blood dripping down my forearm and off my fingers. I could see the knife in my right hand that had given life to the thoughts I had so frequently over the last year or so. I was passing my test - could I do it? I was well on my way as I started up at the top of my forearm, slowly cutting deeper and lower on my arm to push myself. The physical pain of cutting had provided me with a temporary release of the emotional and spiritual pain I had been dealing with for what seemed like a lifetime. And for once, I finally felt like I was in control of something - my life and the ending of it. Until now, everything felt out of control. Nothing made sense, nothing seemed to matter. But finally, with a knife in hand, I had the control to do something, something that finally made sense - a sweet release from this painful life that I was forced into.

I looked back into the fragmented mirror - "How did I get here? How has this happened to me?" This is not what I thought life was supposed to be like. This was certainly not the life that I saw for myself. This was not even the trajectory I was on! Just two years ago, life was great! I was a freshman in high school and in with the popular kids. I was the guy that the other guys wanted to be - I made varsity lacrosse my freshman year and was the only freshman to do it that year. Of course, that made me cooler than anything (at least I felt that way). I was getting older girls, hanging out with the older guys, and going to all the parties. To top it off, I had a 4.0 my first year in and was expecting to do the same my sophomore year. My life felt like a movie and I was the star. But in life, you can be a shooting star or a falling star, and I turned out to be the latter.

As I continued to put blade to flesh for the sake of feeling something more than emotional absence, my girlfriend walked in. Even with the look of absolute horror on her face, she was still the most beautiful girl I had ever laid eyes on - my guardian angel. This is why she was the one who could get me to do anything or stop me from doing anything. It was this love for her and the realization of the pain I was inflicting on her through this horrific act of self harm that got me to stop. I think it's safe to say that it was around this time that I had hit rock bottom.

About two years prior to me acting on the idea and temptation of taking my life, the life of my grandmother was taken. She died of cancer, the four-letter word that too many of us are all too familiar with. Cancer is a cruel mistress. She sneaks up on you. She doesn't care about your situation, your life plans, or your ambitions. She attacks, sometimes without a trace, until you find her living in every corner of your body, literally sucking the life out of you. She looks you dead in the eye, brings you in for a warm embrace, only to stab you in the gut with a dull rusty blade, slowly twisting the knife until you can no longer stand the pain. Then she watches you while you bleed out on the loved ones trying to save you. This is how I felt watching my grandmother slowly slip into the hands of death. It was this painful experience of watching the life of someone I loved, cherished, and adored be ripped from me without sympathy that sent me spiraling downward into a personal hell I almost didn't escape. But, as you can tell from my name on this book, I did. I'm one of the fortunate ones.

My grandmother, Shirley, was a saint in my eyes. That's actually why, after her passing, I immortalized her in my first tattoo, repre-sented by the Mother Mary. Mother Mary was pure, kind, chosen, and gave life to beauty. That was my grandmother to me. She represented those things and more. She was a beautiful warrior who lived up to her maiden name, Wolfe. She led her pack with ferocity and love. Above Mary on my tattoo, however, is the Grim Reaper, which, of course, represents death. He hovers over the top of Mary to remind me that no matter who you are, how pure you are, how much good you do, death will always find you - always reap when it's his time. At least, that's what it used to mean…

Shirley had been in my life since I could remember. Even now when we watch old family videos, she's there. She's pushing me on swings, putting together my Christmas toys, and helping me play with her dogs. In my memories, she's there teaching me how to sew, how to cook (all I remember how to cook is her "scrud" as we would call it), and how to lead. She was fiery, and when she wanted to get something done, you better get out of her way because she was coming for it and there was nothing that was going to stop her. Like I said, she lived up to the Wolfe name (both in the German ferocity and that of the wild dog). My dad got that quality from her. I like to think that I did too. It's those things that we inherit from others that help us immortalize them after they've gone.

Shirley meant a lot to me. And that meaning continued to grow as I did. When I was about 10, my dad moved her (his mom) and his dad out to California from Texas so that he could be closer to them as they aged. My dad is a sweet man like that, especially with his family. With them closer, we saw them all the time. They ended up moving just 10 minutes away from us. We saw them almost every weekend, did family trips, and really made them feel less like an extension of our family and more like our direct family. At least that's how it felt to me. Maybe that's part of why it hurt me so badly when she died.

The happy life I was living up to this point, which was until I was 16, was about to come to an abrupt halt. My family was having a gathering of some sort and all the kids were playing in the backyard. As my grandparents pulled up, I went out to greet them and say hello. When I did, I noticed my grandmother had a Band-Aid on her right shoulder. When I asked what it was, she told me it was nothing and urged me to go back to playing, which, of course, I did. I was 16. How was I supposed to know that something as simple as a bandaid could mean something as urgent as cancer? But, unfortunately, that's exactly what it meant. And it wasn't just cancer, it was stage four melanoma. I was about to find out real quick just what that meant. My playing days were ending.

I should mention that death has always been hard for me to handle. When I was eight, my babysitter, who lived down the street from us, died. One morning, she just didn't wake up. I remember them initially thinking that she had suffocated in her pillow. It was the last time I used a pillow until they found the actual source of her passing - a blood clot in her brain. My mom and I were in Spain at the time visiting her sister. I can still see us in our hotel, hear my mom on the phone with my dad as he told her the news, and feel her sadness as she broke down into tears. I had no idea what to do, but I remember holding her and telling her she was in a better place. Why I said that - I do not know. I was eight and knew nothing about what happened after we died. Maybe I said it because I had just finished my "first communion." I put that in quotations because we definitely were not religious. Perhaps I felt like a religious answer might comfort my mom. But it was then that death first started consuming my thoughts. Where did we come from? Why are we here? What is the purpose of life? Where do we go when we die? I was only eight, but my search for purpose in and of life began here.

The intrigue of death continued as I went through elementary school. I never forgot about my babysitter and how she just up and died. It alarmed me that we could all up and die just the same. I couldn't comprehend how one could go to bed one night "perfectly fine" and just not wake up. It fascinated and tormented me at the same time.

Then 9/11 happened. I can remember exactly where I was, who was with me, and how I felt. I know the entire world felt that way. What shocked me though, was that people were having to decide to be burned alive or jump to their death. Those decisions were something that I couldn't comprehend. I still can't. It seared the image of the falling man into my brain. The sounds of people hitting the buildings around the news casters is something I can still hear, and I wasn't even there. The world will never forget the impact of 9/11, and it certainly left a lasting impression on me.

Then, when I was 11, our fifth-grade teacher gave us an assignment to write something we were passionate about. Some of my fellow students wrote about their dogs, the ocean, or the majestic animals they loved. Not me. I wrote about death. I actually entitled it DEATH. It went like this:

Death is a very scary thing.

You feel like you have lost your wings.

You feel like you could die of pain.

It's all your fault and all your blame.

When someone dies, you can't go on.

You feel just like your heart has gone.

You feel like you could be alone.

You can only speak in monotone.

You don't know what to do or say.

You sit in the corner of a room all day.

You feel like you're in great despair.

You can't do anything but sit and stare.

Death to me, like this poem, had no closure to it. It seemed to exist only to cause those left behind to witness and experience it. For me personally, it became a barbell filled with pain and despair that I could never remove. The weight of death on my shoulders got heavier and heavier the less I understood it. Each experience filled the bar with thoughts of death and continued to weigh on my soul. But up to this point in life, it had never affected me directly, so the weight was bearable. Funny how life changes…

Back to Shirley, stage four Melanoma, certain death with an uncertain time frame. I had only seen the impact of cancer in movies. And in these movies, you never get a true sense of time - a year goes by in two scenes, or 10 minutes can take the whole movie. With my life experience stemming from my viewing experience, I didn't understand what was happening to my grandmother or how much longer she would be with us. To me, she looked fine and healthy. She told everyone she felt fine. What was I missing? What couldn't I feel or sense? What couldn't I see? Well, the answer to that question is a pretty easy one, actually. I couldn't see the havoc that the cancer was wreaking inside her. This havoc would go on for four months. Four months to close out a lifetime. From what I saw and experienced, it was four excruciating months that ended what she called a wonderful life. Four torturous months to end 72 wonderful years. That's all it took.

During those four months, I slowly became numb. So many questions in my head, so many feelings in my heart, and they all remained unanswered. Honestly, I thought they were unanswerable. At 16, I didn't have the tools to communicate what I was going through. No one understood me because I didn't understand myself. I couldn't articulate what was going on inside me, the pain I was feeling, the hopelessness that was consuming me. Because of that, I did the worst thing one could have done, but the only thing that made sense at the time - I distanced myself from everyone. I spent all my time alone. I avoided family meals, family outings, parties with friends, anything that would have forced me to put on a happy face I avoided. I couldn't stand pretending that I was happy when I felt like I was dying inside, and I couldn't understand how people just accepted what was happening. This lack of acceptance changed my trajectory and pushed me off course.

As my grandmother continued to fade away physically, I continued to fade away mentally, emotionally, and spiritually. I felt as if my body remained, but my soul was blowing away in the wind.

My parents eventually moved Shirley into their house. My dad wanted to be there for his mom and my mom offered this as a solution for that. It was very sweet of them to provide my grandmother with such a comfortable place to die. But what they didn't know was that as the house filled with her death, it slowly filled with mine as well. With each stage of her physical death that I witnessed, I glimpsed my own emotional and spiritual death. I'll never forget how hard it was for her to breathe at the end and the pressure that I could feel in my chest as I listened to her struggle. Her heart eventually stopped beating, and as it did, it was as if mine stopped producing the emotions a heart is supposed to produce - love, happiness, joy, empathy. All of that had died with my grandmother. I had become a zombie - a semi functioning human who's void of emotion and purpose. One who wanders until their death comes as continuing decay and deterioration until they literally fall apart. My decaying had been happening for months, but with her passing it accelerated.

Now what? How do I move on from this? How do I find "closure"? How could everyone accept that someone they had literally spent an entire lifetime with was no longer around? And it wasn't just that she died, but she was absolutely tortured! In our house! We let death into our lives and his presence was still palpable where we slept! She died in my parent's room, for goodness' sake! That same room that as a kid I would run to for comfort as my kids now do to mine! Now where was I supposed to turn to refuge, comfort, and escape from pain!? How did anyone move on from any of this!? (I really hope you're putting an emphasis on the exclamation points as you read, because you should be reading with rage - I'm aggressively typing with it).

We traveled back to Texas to lay my grandmother to rest. This was difficult for my dad and his dad, Shirley's husband. Texas was relatively far - not somewhere my grandfather could just visit on a weekend if he missed her. But to them, this was their home. This is where they were born and this is where they wanted to die. I respected it, but I sure didn't understand it. Why would we honor a dead person's last wish? They were dead now… and as my dad told me, "They were just worm food." I wanted her buried close so we could visit her and I could try to wrap my head around letting her go. Something I never got to do, actually. I walked out of the house when it was time to say goodbye. I couldn't do it. I gave up on her. I think me giving up on her also led me to giving up on me. It's something I'll take with me to the grave, I think. Not that it's something I haven't forgiven myself for, but it's a moment that if I could do over and do differently, I absolutely would.

My brothers and I were four of her pallbearers. As if her death wasn't heavy enough, now I had to carry her and bury her in the ground. Something, again, I couldn't seem to wrap my "undeveloped brain" around. Her coffin kept appearing in my mind, breaking under the soil's weight, and worms eating her flesh until only bones were left. It was not how I wanted to picture the grandmother that I loved so much, but that image seemed to burn itself into my brain. Looking back at pictures of us at her funeral, you can see the weight of sadness and confusion I carried with me through the day. My dad even made comments like, "Man, you can really see you were hurting." "You did not handle this well." "This was really hard on you." All I could think when he said this was, "ya think? Too bad you're 15 years too late to recognize it." But that was my anger talking, and that wasn't his fault. He may have been in the pictures with me, but neither he nor my mom could see the pain I was carrying. Like I said, I really didn't know how to tell them, which meant they had no idea what I needed.

Looking through those same pictures, my dad made comments about the flowers that so many people had sent to his mother's funeral. "This is a life lesson I learned that day, Alex. Flowers make everything a little better." He went on about how his company at the time even sent flowers, and that really helped him. Then he said something that blew my mind, my 31-year-old adult mind. He said, "It helped give me closure." There was that word again! The first thought that came to my mind was one filled with rage, something I hadn't really felt since the time these pictures were taken. "CLOSURE! YOU HAD CLOSURE!? YOUR MOTHER WAS JUST PUT IN THE GROUND AND ALL IT TOOK TO GIVE YOU CLOSURE WERE SOME CHEAP FLOW-ERS!? NO WONDER YOU NEVER UNDERSTOOD ME!" I put it in all caps because I thought it in all caps - I felt it in all caps. This was the first time I really understood my dad's disconnect with me, and mine with him - 15 years later…

I think the largest disconnect between us, one of Grand Canyon size proportions, was that of the purpose of this life and what happens next. I can't place all the blame on him for our conversations constantly going astray. After all, I couldn't truly articulate what was going on in my head and heart. I still have problems with it sometimes. But as I asked, "What's next? What happened to Shirley?" He responded with something like, "She's worm food now. Nothing happens next. We live, we die. That's just how life goes." He could be right for all I know, but was that the answer my 16-year-old heart wanted to hear? Absolutely not! Essentially, my dad just told me, "YOLO, kid. Move on." And that's how it was received. The reason that misunderstanding became the size of a global destination was because I couldn't just move on. I couldn't accept that this life was it. "YOLO" was not enough for me. Because if our only purpose in this life was to get to the end, then I could hurry that process myself. If life was a race to this unknown finish line, I could get there faster. All I had to do was take matters into my own hands. And that's exactly what I started doing. Even driving myself to hockey practice, I would take the back roads and drive with the lights off, hoping an "accident" would happen. I'd hit a deer, I'd run off a cliff, someone would crash into me. I was testing the limits of The Reaper, just waiting for him to come collect his bounty. And of course, all of this made me increasingly negative, angry, empty, and with no remorse for my actions and whoever got in my way. This furthered that gap between me and my dad and continued to make things worse.

As this distance increased between my father and me, I tried to rely on my mother. My mom had always been there for me. She was my light in the dark, my heat in the cold, my compass when I wandered. But, as with the rest of the good in my life, it rang true that "all good things must come to an end." I asked my mom the same things I asked of my dad, but still felt empty with the answers she gave me. Her answer was more along the lines of energy and karma - what you give is what you get. While I believe in that, it wasn't enough substance for me to build a foundation of truth on. Again, I needed answers to where we came from, why we are here, and where we were going. My parents didn't seem to have those answers. In fact, they didn't really care to have those answers. This, too, boggled my mind. "To each their own," I guess, but "my own" needed some answers. If I couldn't get those answers from my mom, at least I could rely on her to support me through these dark times… right?

I've always known my mom loves me. That has never been a doubt in my mind. EVER. As kids, my younger brother and I would go grocery shopping with her at our local grocery store, Lucky. As we would ride in the cart with her, begging for all the treats, she would inevitably have to say "no" to as a good parent. We would poke and prod her with questions, as all good kids do to their parents. One of those questions was "how much do you love us?" My mom would respond with the normal answers - "so much!" "More than you could know." "This much!" As she would spread her arms as far as they could go. My brother and I would smile and giggle as we felt the love. One day, she responded to our "how much do you love us question" with the answer that became our family barometer for love. She said, "I love you bigger than Lucky times infinity." This stuck to where my mom, brother, dad, and I all have it tattooed on us now. I have never doubted that my momma loves her boy.

Love is a funny thing, though. It's abstract, invaluable yet un-valuable, used as a metric for emotion and yet immeasurable. How much you love someone is dictated by your daily actions towards them. Are you there when they need you most? Do you stand up for them when they can't fight for themselves? Do you believe in them even if they don't believe in themselves? Do you pick them up when they've fallen to their lowest? Would you give your life in order to save theirs? These can be questions that can help measure the amount of love you have for someone. As sweet as "bigger than Lucky times infinity" is, "I love you enough to stand up for you when you can't stand up for yourself" means more. And that's what I needed. Unbeknownst to me, that is what she was giving me. I just couldn't feel it.

My dad and I continued to enlarge this gap between us and my mom was now stuck in the middle of it. Does she side with her husband, who is saying that their son is broken, unfixable, a burden, and a threat? Or does she side with her son, who is saying that her husband is emotionally and mentally unsupportive? One who couldn't care less about me, and who would be happier if I was gone? I hope I never have to make that decision myself - it's almost an impossible one to make. The side she ended up taking was my father's. Now that I'm a husband, I understand the choice she made. But at 16 when my world was falling apart, it was something that I couldn't wrap my head around. When I figured that out, the lights went out, the warmth disappeared, the compass lost its ability to point north. My last safe haven had been removed from me and I was unquestionably alone.

With my mom no longer on my side, I felt lost. She was the last person I ever would have thought I would lose. Now, with no one to help bolster me, my ability to overcome had diminished. I didn't have the tools and know-how to determine my worth. My worth was always attached to being loved and appreciated by others. Especially my parents. Especially my mom. I always felt like the golden boy, the favorite, the star. But like I said at the beginning, you can either be a shooting star or a falling star… everyone realized now, including myself, that I was falling. And fast.

This was the end of the road for me. I had lost it all. The sports I once loved and valued so much lost their importance. The friends I once turned to for support were now unreachable. I had cut them out. My parents thought I was worthless, broken, under developed, crazy, burdensome, and a threat. And above all (or maybe below all since we're talking rock bottom here), I now thought these things too.

I believed I was broken and not worth healing. That I was insane and unfixable. That I was a burden and everyone would be better off without me. That I held no value, no purpose, and no reason for being. I had reached the end of my race. The finish line was right in front of me. Now it was finally time to cross the line.

---

This book is not an autobiography. I do not mean it to detail the aches and pains of my life. It's not meant to dog anyone or recommend religions. The reason this chapter has been written is to express to you, the reader, that I've hit my rock bottom and I know what genuine pain, depression, anxiety, hopelessness, loss, and lack of self-worth feel like. And I express this so that you can know how powerful the tools are that I share in this book. I still deal with bouts of depression, anxiety, and lack of self worth on an almost daily basis. But with these tools, I control my narrative and the fight within. I make sure I'm living a fulfilled and purposeful life that leads to my definition of success and happiness. THAT is the point and purpose of this book. To show you that if I can use these tools to help dig myself out of the hole I was in and still combat the daily fights I face, you can do the same. I am no one special. I'm not some battle hardened Navy SEAL or a retired Monk. I'm a normal dude who wants to help others overcome themselves in order to become who they have the potential to become. If you apply these practices and principles, I promise that the version of you that you see in the mirror today will be a far better version in six months. And that is what life is all about - making small daily changes to be better than you were yesterday. There's no secret to it - it takes a lot of hard work and dedication. But you are in control of your life, and you truly have the potential within to become whoever you want to become. Take that first step, get to work, and keep moving forward. If you do, you too can become Stronger Than Your Pain.

# CHAPTER 1
## MIND YOUR ROOTS
### "THE HAPPINESS OF YOUR LIFE DEPENDS ON THE QUALITY OF YOUR THOUGHTS." - MARCUS AURELIUS

---

Thoughts are a funny thing if you think about them. Even that is weird - think about the thoughts you're thinking about right now. You're probably thinking, "This dude sure is saying 'think' a lot and we're only in the first paragraph." And you're right. My thought exactly…

Seriously though, thoughts are an enigma. They come to define us, yet no one sees them. They branch out in thousands of directions as they grasp at concepts we're seeking to understand. They're extremely powerful, yet empty unless we feed them. And, over time, they dictate our overall wellbeing.

Our thoughts are much like the roots of a tree. They remain unseen, but they keep the tree grounded. They are what feed the rest of the tree, and what they feed off of is paramount to its health. If the tree is to grow as tall as it can, its roots must run deep and spread wide to secure its stability. When the roots of one tree touch another tree's roots, they have the option to intertwine and grow stronger together or poison each other. Just like a tree, we, too, must MIND our ROOTS.

The straw that broke the camel's back, or my back with what became a suicidal depression, was that I finally gave into what I thought everyone was thinking about me. My friends thought what they thought, but it didn't break me. My dad thought what he thought, but it didn't break me. My mom thought what she thought, but it didn't break me. Sure, it weakened me, especially when it all piled on together, but it didn't break me. What broke me was me finally giving into those thoughts and believing them myself. Oh, what I wish I knew at the time - our thoughts dictate our destiny.

This is the key I wish I had known while dealing with my depression, and one I lean on daily to this day. I'll repeat it - our thoughts dictate our destiny. This lesson is nothing new. In fact, it's 2,500 years old. Lao Tzu gave it to us back in 500 BC. He told us:

# "WATCH YOUR THOUGHTS, FOR THEY BECOME YOUR WORDS. WATCH YOUR WORDS, FOR THEY BECOME YOUR ACTIONS. WATCH YOUR ACTIONS, FOR THEY BECOME YOUR HABITS. WATCH YOUR HABITS, FOR THEY BECOME YOUR CHARACTER. WATCH YOUR CHARACTER, FOR IT BECOMES YOUR DESTINY."

While it's a cycle with many steps, the linear connection is that our thoughts become our destiny. So, if we are to control our destiny, we must learn to control our thoughts.

I call this cycle the Mastery Cycle. Mastery of what? YOU. Yes, reader, you. Congratulations, we can finally say that something does in fact revolve around us! While it's not the world itself, it's everything that we do in it. Who you are dictates your thoughts, and your thoughts dictate who you are. Same with your words and your actions, ultimately leading to your destiny. Don't worry, we'll cover the rest in subsequent chapters.

If we are to control our thoughts, we first have to understand what thoughts are. Why? Because if we're to solve a problem, we first have to understand what the problem is at its root. See what I did there?

We have up to 60,000 thoughts per day. That's a lot. But that's not the crazy part. Of those 60,000 thoughts per day, 95% are repetitive. Our brain just runs on repeat from the day before, and the day before that, and the day before that, and the day before that… you get my point. Even so, that's not the crazy part. The baffling part is that of those 60,000 thoughts per day, 80% are negative. Not only is this baffling, but it's an issue. After all, our thoughts dictate our destiny. If our thoughts are naturally negative, what is to be said about our destiny?

This begs the question - "Why would 80% of our thoughts be negative?" And that's a significant question. One popular theory is that it's because of an evolutionary pattern that kept us alive. Over time, our species as human developed a disposition towards the negative as a survival mechanism. Negativity is far more potent to the brain than positivity. It's sad, but it's true. So over the last hundreds of thousands of years, we have wired our brains to not only focus on the negative, but to remember the negative. We need to change that.

Now, before you think I'm telling you to stop thinking negatively, I want to clarify what I'm saying:

# WE NEED TO CONTROL OUR THOUGHTS AND WHERE WE DIRECT THEM, NOT IGNORE THEM COMPLETELY.

In fact, studies have shown that thinking negatively can be beneficial to us, if used in our CONTROL. Because we are evolutionarily predisposed towards the negative, we can target negative thinking towards situations that we want to avoid in the future. This allows us to gather motivation and determination to act. That's great. Remembering the negative that happened in the past allows us to remember lessons learned so we know how to better act when they arise in the future. Again, that's great. We need that. The key, as with anything, is to remain in control, especially when using negative thinking to our advantage.

Here's the thing about thoughts - in and of themselves, they have no power. They are empty. That's why we can have so many in a day or at a time. When something happens to us or someone around us, we have many thoughts that occur simultaneously. Just because we have up to 60,000 thoughts per day doesn't mean that we're aware of all 60,000 or that they all take hold. So which ones take hold? Well, now, that is up to you. Or at least it should be.

Like the roots of a tree need to be fed to grow, so, too, do our thoughts. And what do thoughts feed off of? Our emotions. Of the 60,000 thoughts that we have per day, the ones that take hold and define us are the ones that we assign emotions to. Let me rephrase that.

# OF THE 60,000 THOUGHTS WE HAVE PER DAY, THE ONES THAT TAKE HOLD ARE THE ONES THAT GET AN EMOTION ASSIGNED TO THEM.

The difference in those statements is whether you're the one doing the assigning of the emotion or the emotion is being assigned automatically by the situation itself. While it's subtle, it's destiny defining.

If we are not actively taking control of our thoughts, then our thoughts are actively taking control of us. They do this by feeding off of whatever emotion is chosen as a response. Take social media, for example. You can scroll through your feed and one photo makes you happy, the next makes you sad, the next makes you jealous, the next fills you with rage, and because you can't end on a rage filled post, you continue to scroll until you find another one that makes you happy. With those emotions fueled from external and often fake experiences of others, comes thoughts of, "I wish I was doing that," "Why can't I be that pretty or that fit," "Why can't I have a nice car or six-pack like that"? Then, for the rest of the day, we remain on an emotional roller coaster until we get our next bump of happiness from some social drug we're addicted to. I don't know about you, but that doesn't sound like control of thought or destiny to me.

If our thoughts feed off of our emotions, we have to learn to interrupt the cycle of emotional assignment. We must also learn control which emotions we decide to feed our thoughts. This is where we can begin to control our Mastery Cycle. Now we have to answer the question of how…

When something happens to us, and life always happens to us, we can have one of two responses. One, respond with a knee-jerk reaction. Or, two, we can take a step back with the idea in mind that we want to control our reaction. Knee-jerk frequently turns into ME-jerk, because immediate responses are usually ones we wish we could take back. We want to avoid ME-jerk reactions. Taking a step back creates space between what happened to us - the stimulus, and our reaction - the response. Between stimulus and response is where we get to choose which emotion we want to assign as our reaction. The greater the distance we can create, the more time we allow for our response, the more control we'll have. Over time and with practice, we can extend the gap between stimulus and response much faster, allowing for better control in less time. Taking control of our response allows us to choose, and having the ability to choose for ourselves is the greatest act of freedom. On the contrary, knee-jerk reactions to the stimulus in life make us a slave to our emotions because it has immediately removed our ability to choose how we want to react and feel.

STiMULUS _____CONTROL_____ RESPONSE

Regarding our feelings, we must realize that they are often big, fat liars. When someone cuts you off in traffic and your immediate reaction is to want to punch that dude in the face, is that really the best reaction to that situation? No. It's not. Just let it go! Take a step back and have some perspective that maybe that guy simply made a mistake and didn't see you. Or he's driving his child to the hospital and has to get over really quickly. Or he's simply just an a-hole, and just because he's an a-hole doesn't mean you should be one, too. Your feelings are liars most of the time because they don't reflect how you really feel over time, but simply how you feel at the moment.

# DON'T MAKE PERMANENT DECISIONS BASED ON TEMPORARY FEELINGS.

In most cases, feelings are temporary, and if analyzed for over five minutes, you can see that.

In today's world, however, our feelings tend to run the show. Everyone is driven by their feelings and entitled to their emotions. While that's true - you are entitled to your feelings - no one else is entitled to them. If you're entitled to your own feelings, then that means that everyone is entitled to their own feelings, and if people feel differently about something, it implies that someone will have to change their feelings for someone else, and that never works. So…. We need to look beyond our feelings and realize that they change, and therefore should not be the sole determining variable in our equation of life.

Here is a cheesy motivational parlor trick, but drives the point home. Let's assign a value to each letter in the alphabet based on its place within. Therefore, A=1, B=2, C=3, and so on. The goal is to get what we pay attention to, or assign our emotions to, to equal out to 100%. Here's an example:

- KNOWLEDGE = 11+14+15+23+12+5+4+7+5=96%. Cool - makes sense. The saying "knowledge is power" can hold water here. But I always argue that "knowledge is power, only when applied." The application of that knowledge is hard work. Let's look at that…

- HARD WORK = 8+1+18+4+23+15+18+11=98%. Outstanding. We're getting closer. I'd be fine saying that hard work is the key to success. But if there is room to improve, let's seek after it.

Let's look at our FEELINGS, since today that is what we assign most of our value to:

- FEELINGS = 6+5+5+12+9+14+7+19=77%. For this completely non-scientific example, our feelings only amount to 77%. Quite frankly, I would agree that they amount to much less than that, but we'll continue to drive the point home.

Now I want to focus on something that is well within our control at all times. This thing comprises our emotions and is something that, regardless of how we feel in any moment, we can come back to. That is our attitude.

- ATTITUDE = 1+20+20+9+20+21+4+5=100%. BOOM. Fake motivational math for the win. Our attitude is 100% what we should focus on as a starting place to gain control of our thoughts, followed by everything else. Turns out that our parents are actually right about something. Go figure.

STIMULUS     CONTROL     RESPONSE

WHAT DO WE REALLY HAVE
CONTROL OVER?

WE CONTROL OUR ATTITUDE [100%] WE CONTROL OUR
THOUGHTS & FEELINGS = REALTIONS

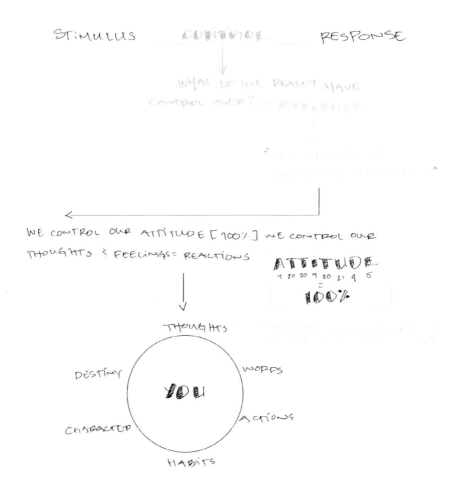

ATTITUDE
1 20 20 9 20 21 4 5
=
100%

THOUGHTS

DESTINY     YOU     WORDS

ACTIONS

CHARACTER

HABITS

# WE DEFINE OUR ATTITUDE AS "A SETTLED WAY OF THINKING OR FEELING ABOUT SOMEONE OR SOMETHING, TYPICALLY ONE THAT IS REFLECTED IN A PERSON'S BEHAVIOR."

While I root this example in nothing but philosophical metaphors and motivation tactics, it works because it's true. Our attitude is the first thing that we can control that gives us the ability to control our thoughts and ourselves. Looking at ancient texts, we can analyze great thought leaders who took the approach of controlling their attitudes using mantras - things they would tell themselves that reflected their attitude in times of hardship:

- Jesus: Thy will be done. Jesus was aligning what happened around him to the will of God. What ever happened, happened and he would face it with a respectful attitude and be grateful for it. Attitude = THY WILL BE DONE.

- Marcus Aurelius: Memento Mori - Remember Death. You are going to die eventually. We all are. So live each day as if it's your last and be grateful for each breath you take. You should celebrate and not take for granted the fact that you're alive and breathing. Attitude = MEMENTO MORI.

- Epictetus: Amor Fati - Love Fate. Epictetus, having been a slave for many years, advises us to love fate. Control what you can and let go of what you can't, for fate will happen regardless. "Do not seek for things to happen the way you want them to; rather, wish that what happens happens the way it happens: then you will be happy." Attitude = AMORI FATI.

Why use a mantra to help center themselves and control their attitude? It's actually pretty straightforward…

## MANTRA, WHEN BROKEN DOWN, ACTUALLY MEANS "TOOL OF THE MIND."

In Sanskrit, 'manas' means mind, and 'tra' means tool. Mantra directly translates to "mind tool." Each one of these examples of attitude towards life has given us a mantra to live by. One that we can use in times of hardship to remind us to control our attitude, for that is all we can truly control. What is your mantra that helps you determine your attitude towards life? If you don't have a mantra yet, borrow one of these above. Let them help you frame your attitude so you can frame your thoughts.

While this is easily said, it's much harder to do. Just because we tell ourselves something doesn't mean it's going to change our mindset. We'll discuss that more in the subsequent chapters. However, this is a crucial place to start. We live in a world of thought. Our thoughts create our experiences, and therefore, we experience what we think. If we're constantly thinking in the negative, that is what we're going to experience. But if we're thinking in the positive, that is what we're going to find in life. It really comes down to that.

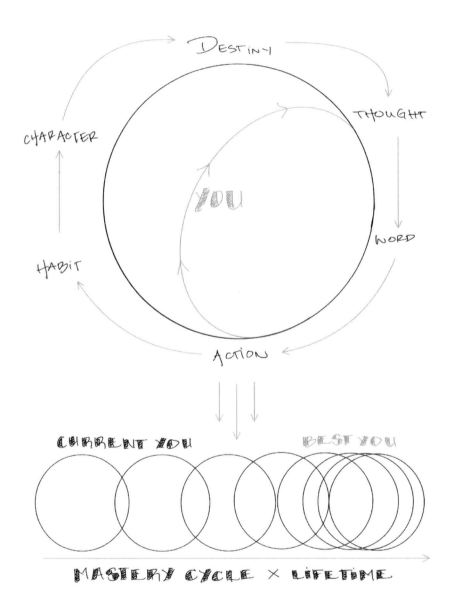

# "AS A MAN THINKS, SO HE IS; AS HE CONTINUES TO THINK, SO HE REMAINS."

James Allen nailed it. We need to mind our thoughts and continue to mind them at all times, for that determines who we become.

This practice is one that is to be done, not with an end in mind, but until we approach our end. Regardless of where you are in life, your status, your experience, or your "enlightenment," there is always room to improve. This Mastery Cycle develops as we do, and as our thoughts improve, so does the version of the person at the center. As that person improves, so do our thoughts, which then leads to further improvement of self. This is a wonderful message of hope - our destiny is in our hands at all times and we can direct it simply by controlling our thoughts, at least as a starting place.

Whether we're reframing our thoughts to grab hold of our emotions and feelings to better control our attitude, or reframing our thoughts to think negatively for a moment with the purpose of avoiding a negative outcome, the point in all of it is to learn to control our thoughts. Recognize that they are mostly negative because of our evolution and don't let that get you down, for in and of themselves, thoughts have no power. Thoughts derive their power from our emotions and feelings. Those emotions and feelings can either come in a ME-Jerk reaction, or it can come as a controlled reaction as we control the space between stimulus and response.

How can we gain control over that space? We can check our attitude, for that is something that we truly have control over. And since our attitude is a settled way of thinking or feeling, when we control our attitude, we control not only our thoughts, but our feelings that feed them. You can control your destiny and who you become by simply learning to control your thoughts. Moral of the story? MIND YOUR ROOTS.

# CHAPTER ACTIVITY
## CREATE YOUR MANTRA

---

We discussed the need for a mantra that you can repeat to yourself in times of hardship, like philosophers of the past and thought leaders of the present. This activity it to help you create your own so that you can grab control of your thoughts by leaning on something meaningful to you. This will help you control your attitude - your way of thinking or feeling. Ipso facto, mantra — attitude adjustment — thought control.

Let's start with an example of how this works by using something my wife and I are teaching our children now. The mantra that we're teaching our daughters is,

## "I'M STRONGER THAN MY PAIN."

Hence the title of this book. Here's how it's applied.

Whether our daughter has stubbed her toe on the corner of the couch as she's running around the room, bonks her head on the corner of the kitchen island as she dances in the kitchen, or has an emotional boo boo from a friend at school (she's four so boo boos happen all the time) we deploy the Mantra. First, we acknowledge what's happened with a, "Hey babe, that sucks. I know that hurts. I'm so sorry. But ya know what, crying about it isn't going to help, so let's focus on what can. Let's take some deep breaths and breathe through this." This allows our four-year-old to separate herself between the stimulus, a bonked head or emotional boo boo, and the response, the wailing and gnashing of teeth. After she takes a few deep breaths and calms down enough to talk through her tears and snot, we say, "Okay, now tell me your mantra. What do you say when you get hurt?" She'll respond through controlled whimpers, "I'm, stronger, than, my, pain." We'll make her say it three times, each time getting louder and louder, until at the final time, we have her scream it - "I'M STRONGER THAN MY PAIN!" This puts her in a silly attitude and allows her to move away from the stimulus in the moment and move towards controlling her attitude - thoughts and feelings - so she can go play again.

If this tool can help our four-year-old daughter, it can help us as adults. Honestly, I've taken what my wife and I teach our daughters and applied it to my life. Whenever I feel emotionally broken down, I take some deep breaths, gather myself, and tell myself, "I'm stronger than my pain." Then I can imagine my daughter picking herself up and driving forward, and I become determined to do the same.

What is something that your parents, mentors, or support network have taught you that comes to your mind every time you get frustrated, sad, anxious, or depressed? What is something you say to yourself to amp yourself up when you're feeling down or about to go compete in your sport? What is that consistent saying in your life that is your go-to for personal internal motivation? That is what we need to use as the anchor for your mantra. Let's break it down into three easy steps:

- Write about your biggest accomplishments so far. Aim for 5-10. Don't be modest about it. You earned these accomplishments, so be proud and write them down.

- Focus on your thoughts about these accomplishments. How did they make you feel? What was your attitude like when you accomplished them?

- Condense those feelings of accomplishment and success into a word or phrase. That is YOUR mantra. Now use this as your go-to saying to re-center yourself and gain control of your thoughts and attitude as often as needed.

My personal anchor is THE ONE YOU FEED. When something happens to me, the quickest way for me to grab hold of my thought process is to tell myself, "Alex, focus on THE ONE YOU FEED." Most of the time, it leads to, "Alright man, THE ONLY WAY OUT IS THROUGH, so nut up and get moving." It sets the mind towards what is controllable and actionable, allowing me to continue to progress. It grounds me and helps me feed my roots to keep the rest of my tree healthy.

Turn inward and study yourself to see what you can use as your mantra to grab hold of your thoughts by controlling your attitude. Find your mantra and use it as the super food to MIND YOUR ROOTS. Maybe that's one you can use right there...

# CHAPTER 2
## BECOME A SUBJECTIVE SPECTATOR
### "RAISE YOUR WORDS, NOT YOUR VOICE. IT IS RAIN THAT GROWS FLOWERS, NOT THUNDER." - RUMI

There's a monster living inside me. While it has no defined shape, it seems to closely resemble me. Its eyes pierce my soul. His dark, cloak-like figure is constantly and erratically shifting, so I can never grab hold of him. His teeth are like fangs, with a jaw that can unhinge in order to consume my heart and soul in one bite. I can feel his claws tearing at my chest as he tries to find a way out into the world. I can tell he wants out - he needs out. My body is his prison. My chest aches from the pressure of him pushing against my ribs. When that doesn't work, he tries to make his way up my throat, thrashing as he gives everything he has to climb up and out of my mouth. My throat feels as if I'm swallowing red-hot needles fresh from the fiery forge as his claws shred my esophagus. When the monster realizes he can't escape, he continues to climb, scratch, push, punch his way up. His method of escape now is to break me with sheer force, like frozen water pops a can - from the inside. He ends up in my head, in my mind. He's resilient in his mission to find a way out.

My head now feels like it's splitting as his figureless body thrashes around my head, his presence being far too large for the space he now consumes. Finally, he realizes I won't allow him to enter the world. If people saw him, saw what lives within me, they would never accept me or show me love. I can't let him out. With this realization, his physical thrashing slows, and he begins to settle. Not only does he settle his movement, but he settles his presence. He makes a home of my mind, of my mental space. This monster now lives in my head, still doing all he can to accomplish his mission – get out into the world. But now, rather than trying to physically rip his way through me, he uses me as his vehicle to accomplish his mission – wreak havoc and destruction wherever he goes. For if he does that, he'll escape through me, and that will be enough.

His tactic now becomes soft whisperings of failure, worthlessness, lack of purpose, and loss of love. His goal is to isolate me from the world through my perspective of nothingness. This monster, the savage he is, is now one of my closest and longest relationships. He has homesteaded my mind.

After years of fighting, I could no longer differentiate his whispers from my thoughts. He had become me, and I him. His mumblings of, "You're good for nothing. No one loves you. You're worthless. In fact, you're even less than worthless. You're a burden. You're a waste of space. You're not worthy of the air you breathe. Everyone would be better off without you," were my thoughts that became my reality. He had gained complete control of me. His figureless, undefined shape was what I saw in the mirror. I, too, was figureless and undefined, splintered and shattered. Physically, mentally, emotionally, spiritually figureless, undefined, and shattered. What was once his prison was now his playground. This monster had achieved his goal. He had made it out into the world. I had lost the battle of trying to hide him from everyone. The world now looked this monster in the eyes, only to them, they saw me. I was finished. Alex became a bag of flesh and bones controlled by this monster within. I was the mask he wore to roam round the world. Alex and this monster were now one. I was now the one in prison.

---

This was me at my lowest point. This monster had taken control. After years of fighting the urges to let him out, he consumed me. Fortunately, while he almost won the war for my life, he didn't. And in the process, I learned a lot of tools to deal with him and become myself.

Almost all of us have a monster within us. It may not be as vicious as mine. It may not feel like mine does, but it's there. It's that little voice that tells you that you can't, that you're not good enough, that you're not worthy of love or accomplishment. It's the one that stops you from giving it your all when you know you can give more. It's the one that fills you with fear and holds you back from achieving what you know you're capable of. Most importantly, it's the one that stops you from becoming who you are fully capable of becoming. That's because the more growth you get internally, the larger you become internally, the smaller he gets. Your monster cannot live with losing his influence over you. This is exactly why we must develop the tools to tame it.

Here's this biggest point we have to take home regarding your inner monster:

# WHILE HE LIVES WITHIN US, HE DOES NOT DEFINE US. WE ARE NOT OUR MONSTERS. WE ARE NOT OUR NEGATIVITY.

Sure, that ignoramus lives within us, but we are not it and it is not us. But in order to ensure that, we have to know how to separate ourselves from it, from our negativity. And that takes some work, as any superb skill does.

Learning to separate ourselves from our inner monster - our negativity within - is what I call becoming a Subjective Spectator.

# SUBJECTIVE SPECTATING IS WHEN WE REMOVE OURSELVES FROM THE FIRST PERSON PERSPECTIVE OF WHAT WE'RE EXPERIENCING, TAKING A SPECTATOR'S PERSPECTIVE OF THE SITUATION.

In the case of separating ourselves from the negative, this allows us to see ourselves and the situation from an outsider's view. The goal is to remove the knee-jerk (often leading to a ME-jerk) reaction that comes with first-person experience to help us make a more thoughtful reaction. This Subjective Spectator perspective considers, as much as possible, the complete story. This includes the first-person view and the view of others involved in the experience.

This tool of Subjective Spectating is extremely important because it allows us to manage our own thoughts, also known as meta-cognition. Metacognition is an awareness of one's thought processes and can help define the patterns behind them.

# USING THIS SUBJECTIVE SPECTATING TOOL CAN HELP US DO EXACTLY WHAT WE TALKED ABOUT IN THE PREVIOUS CHAPTER - CONTROLLING OUR ATTITUDE AND, THEREFORE, OUR THOUGHTS, BY REVIEWING OUR THOUGHTS THEMSELVES.

From there, we can decide which type of attitude we'd like to have with the ultimate goal of being in complete control of the one thing we actually have control over - ourselves.

Addressing the Mastery Cycle, we need to watch our thoughts because they become our words. But which words do our thoughts become? That, my friend, is a great question.

Words are a funny thing. They can move us with poetry and music. They can motivate us with quotes and catchy phrases. And yet, at the same time, we try to discount them. "Actions speak louder than words." That's true, but that shouldn't discount the value of the words, it should emphasize the potency of the action. "Sticks and stones may break my bones, but words will never hurt me." Again, that's true, but the "never hurt me part" is more our decision on how to take those words. Words do hurt. Words can kill. Not as fast as one action can, sure, but they can kill. Words kill via 1,000 paper cuts. They are powerful, and we need to give them credit where credit is due.

Back to the Mastery Cycle - our thoughts become our words. Again, which words? Often, we think of our words as only the words that we speak to others - our external communication. But what about the words we use with ourselves? What about our internal communication - how we speak to ourselves?

# TO UNDERSTAND OUR OWN IDENTITY, VALUE, AND PURPOSE, I ARGUE THAT THOSE WORDS ARE FAR MORE IMPORTANT THAN WHAT WE SAY TO OTHERS.

Our external words typically (hopefully) go through some kind of filter. Hopefully, you think about how what you're going to say is going to affect the person you're going to say it to. Most of the time, that is true for most people. We do this because, on some level, we care about that person's feelings and don't want to be a jerk by telling them the cold hard truth bluntly. There is a good way to deliver a message and a bad way, and most of us take that into consideration when speaking to others. But how about when speaking to ourselves?

Let's take, for example, how you would speak to a friend about their personal growth. You may say something like, "Hey friend-o, I know you've got these goals, but I haven't seen you working towards them lately. How are things going? Is there anything that I can do to help? I believe in you and know you can do this. I know how important these goals are for you, so I'm going to keep encouraging you to reach for them because I know you can do it and I know you should do it. You got this!" That's kind, uplifting, and still gets the point across - you're not making progress like you said you wanted to.

Now let's look at how that same message is often said to ourselves. "Hey you worthless wretch, you set these goals and you're nowhere near reaching them. What is wrong with you?" I'd say there is a bit of a difference there. But why?

When we speak to others, there is an immediate judgement that comes with what we say and how we say it. If you spoke to your friend the same way you spoke to yourself using the example above, your friend would punch you in the throat if they held any personal value. But when we speak to ourselves, there is no one but us to judge. And since we're the culprit, that judgement often goes unpunished. This is how words to ourselves kill via 1,000 paper cuts. The death is usually a version of our own. Whether it's in the worst form (suicide rates are increasing year over year), or a subtler form of not living to our fullest potential. We need to have personal integrity and think about how we speak with ourselves. Enter Subjective Spectating.

As we learn to take a step back and separate ourselves from our negativity, we gain a new perspective of self. A few things go into this. First, with this separation, we can see not only ourselves as we are, but our negativity for what it is. Now we can name it. And we should.

Many studies have been done to illustrate the power of self-talk. The biggest underlying message across these various studies is that we do, in fact, need to separate from ourselves in the moment and speak to ourselves as if someone else is speaking to us. That comes as what these studies call "non-first person perspective," or Subjective Spectating. What it means by non-first person is that we can speak to ourselves in either second-person, "you", or third-person, your own name. I'd like to take it a step further and add that not only do we need to view ourselves in a "non-first person" light, but view our negativity as such, addressing it by its name, one that we give it.

This approach, while not previously having any scientific basis behind it, has been passed down for generations. My mom passed it to me, and her mom to her, in the Tale of Two Wolves. It goes like this:

One day a Cherokee Chief takes his grandson fishing. After a while, his grandson becomes frustrated that he hasn't caught anything. Being the wise man that he is, the Chief takes this opportunity to teach his grandson a life lesson.

*"I have a fight going on in me," the old man said. "It's taking place between two wolves. One is evil – he is anger, envy, sorrow, regret, greed, arrogance, self-pity, guilt, resentment, inferiority, lies, false pride, superiority, and ego."*

*The grandfather looked at the grandson and went on. "The other embodies positive emotions. He is joy, peace, love, hope, serenity, humility, kindness, benevolence, empathy, generosity, truth, compassion, and faith. Both wolves are fighting to the death. The same fight is going on inside you and every other person, too."*

*The grandson took a moment to reflect on this. At last, he looked up at his grandfather and asked, "Which wolf will win?"*

*The old Cherokee gave a slight smile and simply replied, "THE ONE YOU FEED."*

This story was passed down to me and has been a part of my life since I was a young boy. My mother would always ask me, "Alex, which wolf are you feeding?" Whenever I would have anxiety, anger, depression, fear, or any emotion that would feed the Evil Wolf, my mom would ask me that question. Then, my mom took it a step further and gave me the same advice I'm giving you now - name that Evil Wolf so you can separate yourself from him / her. This is the monster within all of us. My Evil Wolf's name is Buster, and he's a relentless savage.

Naming our Evil Wolf allows us to separate ourselves from him and tame his wild and careless nature. We Name Him to Tame Him. While this tool was given to me as a gift from my wise mother, it's since been studied and backed by science. Dan Siegel, M.D. is a clinical professor of psychiatry at the UCLA School of Medicine and executive director of the Mindsight Institute, and coined the phrase

Name It to Tame It. Psychologist David Rock expands on Siegel's approach by saying:

## "WHEN YOU EXPERIENCE SIGNIFICANT INTERNAL TENSION AND ANXIETY, YOU CAN REDUCE STRESS BY UP TO 50% BY SIMPLY NOTICING AND NAMING YOUR STATE."

As we note which wolf is being fed within, we acknowledge our thoughts - step one. As we name the state and converse with this wolf as a Subjective Spectator we immediately flow into step two - controlling our words. It's beginning to come together.

Now that we've recognized the fight within, given our Evil Wolf a name, and acknowledged that we can converse with him, we can truly become Subjective Spectators to our negativity within. Don't judge (or do, I can't control you), but I'll give you a personal example of what Subjective Spectating looks like as I converse with Buster. This is the conversation I have with him almost every morning when I sit down at my desk to write. Man, this guy is such an a-hole…

*Alex: "Okay, what do I need to do next?"*

*Buster: "You worthless burden, you need to give up. That's what you need to do next."*

*Alex: "That sure escalated quickly. Where did that come from?"*

*Buster: "You're realizing that you, in fact, have no idea what you're doing. You're not a writer. You're wasting your time. No one will read this book. And those that do won't like it. Like I said, next step is to quit."*

*Alex: "Wow. Maybe you're right. This is way harder than I thought. And I'm definitely not a writer. Why am I even doing this?"*

*Buster: "You're doing this because you're selfish and want attention. If you were a better man, you'd stay in the shadows and live a quiet life without the spotlight."*

*Alex: "Is that true? Is that really what I want out of this?"*

*Buster: "Of course it is. Everything you do, you do for you. All you want is fame, money, and attention to fill the hole in your soul. You don't really want to help anyone. All you want to do is help yourself."*

*Alex: "ENOUGH! Forget you, Buster. If this book will help one person, then I've done enough. I don't want fame or glory. I want to help people learn how to overcome you and live better lives. Sure, I'm not a writer, but I believe in my message, and I've seen how it can change lives first hand. This conversation is over."*

At this point, you're probably ready to put the book down and burn it because you've realized that I'm some dude with multiple personalities telling you how to fight internal demons. While you're not wrong, science backs the approach. So while I'm crazy, I'm justifiably so.

Before I share some studies that back all of this, I want to acknowledge one more thing - there is another wolf within us we need to name. If we're taking the time and energy to name the Evil Wolf within, we should acknowledge the Good Wolf within with the same, if not more, energy and focus.

# IF WE NAME TO TAME OUR EVIL WOLF, WE SHOULD NAME TO AIM OUR GOOD WOLF. AIM HIM TOWARDS WHAT? WHO WE WANT TO BECOME - THE BEST VERSION OF OURSELVES.

Again, I know I sound crazy when I say this, but we should give a name to the Good Wolf that represents the best version of us. This will allow us to continue to take a Subjective Spectator approach to our self-talk, allowing us to further control our Mastery Cycle. The name I have given my Good Wolf, creatively enough, is Alexander Wolfe, and he is the best version of me.

I named Alexander Wolfe as an homage to my late grandmother, Shirley Wolfe (her maiden name). She was the grandmother who's passing led to my approach to suicide. Alexander Wolfe reminds me now that while her passing was difficult, I should live a life worthy of her memory, not one she would be ashamed to watch. Like I said - the best version of me.

To give you an example of how I deploy Wolfe in times of need, let's go back to the conversation with Buster:

*Buster: "Of course it is. Everything you do, you do for you. All you want is fame, money, and attention to fill the hole in your soul. You don't really want to help anyone. All you want to do is help yourself."*

*Alex: "ENOUGH! Forget you, Buster. If this book will help one person, then I've done enough. I want to help people learn how to overcome you and live better lives. Sure, I'm not a writer, but I believe in my message, and I've seen how it can change lives first hand. This conversation is over."*

After I say my last words to Buster, Wolfe chimes in.

*Wolfe: "Nice work, Alex. Way to stand up to Buster and for what you believe in. You're right - you may not be a writer now, but the only way that you'll become one is if you continue to pursue your passion. You may not know what you're doing now, but stopping won't teach you anything. You're doing the right thing, my friend. Keep on this path and give into the process. The outcome will happen as long as you don't quit. You got this."*

Wolfe allows me to become a Subjective Spectator in a positive light. He is all the things the Cherokee Chief describes as the Good Wolf. He supports me, he encourages me, and he sets me straight and lovingly rebukes when it's needed. He is what allows me to converse with myself where I control my words to really take hold of the Mastery Cycle. Alexander Wolfe is my best friend within.

# AFTER ALL, THE RELATIONSHIP WE HAVE WITH OURSELVES IS THE LONGEST, MOST AUTHENTIC AND RAW RELATIONSHIP WE'LL EVER HAVE. WE SHOULD MAKE SURE WE DO EVERYTHING WE CAN TO MAKE THAT RELATIONSHIP A GOOD ONE.

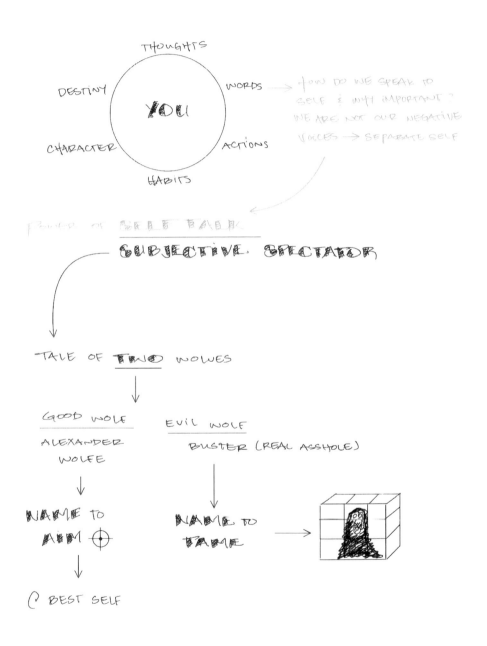

THOUGHTS

DESTINY

YOU

WORDS → HOW DO WE SPEAK TO
SELF & WHY IMPORTANT ?
WE ARE NOT OUR NEGATIVE
VOICES → SEPARATE SELF

CHARACTER

ACTIONS

HABITS

POWER OF SELF TALK

SUBJECTIVE SPECTATOR

TALE OF TWO WOLVES

GOOD WOLF

ALEXANDER
WOLFE

EVIL WOLF

BUSTER (REAL ASSHOLE)

NAME TO
AIM ⊕

NAME TO
TAME →

BEST SELF

From here, the goal is to prove to you that I'm not some crazy schizo and that these methods of self-talk are actually based in science. I know they are because the voices in my head told me that they are… Just kidding. Or am I?

---

The third-person perspective of Subjective Spectating has been studied on some of the highest performing people in the world - professional athletes. If you look at what goes into being a professional athlete, it hits on many, if not all, of the stressors known to humanity. They have to deal with physical performance in front of millions of people. They maintain their contracts based on their daily performance within their teams. After each game, they have to speak in front of thousands, if not millions, of people on television. What they say and do is then played back repeatedly on TV networks and social media platforms. They have to be extremely disciplined in their workouts, sleep, food, and overall energy. They are constantly being berated by "haters." Yet, they are required to show up and perform on a daily and weekly basis. It's no wonder that we idolize these people. They overcome our deepest fears and accomplish our deepest desires. So let's poke and prod at their psyche to see what makes them tick, shall we?

The poking and prodding has been done to study how speaking to yourself in non-first-person dialogue affects performance across all modes of time - past, present, and future. Let's start with the past and make our way to the future.

When we think about something that happened to us in the past, mainly something rather traumatic (like the passing of my grandmother), we think of our experience in the first person. "It hurt so much when I went through that." "I felt so angry when that happened." "I was so distraught that I eventually became numb and felt completely absent." Reflecting in this first-person perspective brings us back to the event, and also the feelings associated with it. This often leads to rumination, a thought process that leads to us dwelling on negative feelings or distress and their causes and consequences.

# THIS HAPPENS BECAUSE REMAINING IN THE FIRST-PERSON KEEPS US FOCUSED ON THE "WHY" OF THE EVENT RATHER THAN THE "WHAT" - WHY DID THIS HAPPEN VS. SIMPLY ACKNOWLEDGING WHAT HAPPENED.

The "why", which often can never be answered, can be a prompt that we need to remove ourselves from the first-person perspective.

A study titled, "Optimizing the Perceived Benefits and Health Outcomes of Writing About Traumatic Life Events[1]" was conducted to understand the effects of third-person perspective on overcoming past traumas. Their goal was not only to see how differing perspectives affected the participants' intrusive thinking as they wrote, but how it helped them over time. Before we break down the study, we need to define Intrusive Thinking / Intrusive Thoughts:

# INTRUSIVE THOUGHTS ARE UNWANTED THOUGHTS THAT CAN POP INTO OUR HEADS WITHOUT WARNING. THEY'RE OFTEN REPETITIVE, WITH THE SAME THOUGHT CROPPING UP AGAIN AND AGAIN, AND THEY CAN BE DISTURBING OR EVEN DISTRESSING.

These are the 80% of our 60,000 thoughts per day that invade our headspace without notice. Simply put, they're Buster. That swine. Moving forward.

44 undergrad students were asked to think about a traumatic or highly stressful event that happened to them in the past. They were then instructed to write about that event in three, 20 minute writing sessions. In their writing, they were asked to be very honest in expressing their deepest thoughts and feelings around this event. This writing exercise was done over four days, allowing for one writing session per day with the opportunity to miss one day if needed. They then split the 44 young adults into two groups - a first-person writing group and a third-person writing group. Each group was given the following instructions:

- *First-Person Group: For the next 20 minutes, I would like for you to write about the event / topic you specified at the beginning of the experiment. In your writing, I'd like you to really let go and explore your very deepest emotions and thoughts. All of your writing will be completely confidential. Don't worry about the spelling or grammar. PLEASE USE THE FIRST-PERSON PERSPECTIVE WHILE WRITING (i.e., instead of saying "He / she thought/ felt…," say "I thought / felt."). In other words, write so that it is clear that the event happened to you.*

- *Third-Person Group: For the next 20 minutes, I would like for you to write about the event / topic you specified at the beginning of the experiment. In your writing, I'd like you to really let go and explore your very deepest emotions and thoughts. All of your writing will be completely confidential. Don't worry about the spelling or grammar. PLEASE USE THE THIRD-PERSON PERSPECTIVE WHILE WRITING (i.e., instead of saying "I thought / felt…," say "He / she thought / felt.").* In other words, *write as if your event happened to someone else.*

Initially, they concluded that first and third-person creative writing were perceived to be equally beneficial. This was surprising due the hypothesis at the beginning of the study. That being that taking a third-person perspective to address past traumas would be more effective in helping to overcome it and combating intrusive thinking. But as the participants returned to finish the study, what they found was much more exciting. A month later, the participants came back to share how their writing assignments had stuck with them. To quote the study, the findings:

## "SIMILARLY REVEALED THAT THIRD-PERSON WRITERS EVIDENCED A POSITIVE (THOUGH MARGINAL) ASSOCIATION BETWEEN BASELINE INTRUSIVE THINKING AND PERCEIVED VALUE / MEANING, WHEREAS FIRST-PERSON WRITERS DISPLAYED A NEGATIVE ASSOCIATION."

This means that not only did third-person writing lead to benefits, but that first-person writing, over time, actually led to a negative impact on the participant's health. This was most likely because of rumination being caused by the review of the past trauma from a first-person perspective.

To officially conclude, the study shared its final verdict:

# "THIS STUDY ADDED TO EXISTING THEORETICAL KNOWLEDGE ABOUT SOCIAL-COGNITIVE THEORY BY PROVIDING EVIDENCE THAT THIRD-PERSON EXPRESSIVE WRITING CAN ACTUALLY REVERSE (RATHER THAN MERELY BUFFER) THE NEGATIVE IMPACT OF INTRUSIVE THINKING ON HEALTH. IN PARTICULAR, THIRD-PERSON WRITERS WITH HIGH LEVELS OF INTRUSIVE THINKING [A BUSTER THAT WON'T SHUT UP] ACTUALLY SHOWED GAINS IN HEALTH ACROSS THE FOLLOW-PERIOD RELATIVE TO FIRST-PERSON EXPRESSIVE WRITERS."

Subjective Spectating, as illustrated in this writing experiment, is proven to help us address past traumas as we view our experience from a third-person perspective. I also suggest that in this process, we view it from the eyes of our Good Wolf - our best selves - to help us aim at truly addressing the situation from a distance. As the third-party group was instructed to write about the experience in the he / she manner, we can expand on that and write about it, or speak to ourselves, from the viewpoint of our best selves. Since this inner version of ourselves is our biggest supporter, he or she can help support you as you reflect.

To give you an example, I've recorded a conversation I've had between myself and Alexander Wolfe. You can't call me crazy now, because science says I'm normal.

As I was sitting at my computer at home on a work call, my wife came barging into my office. I couldn't hear anything, so I slowly looked over to see what was happening just outside my door. My wife was standing there, a reddish purple face, eyes strained, shoulders slumped forward. She was choking. I shot into action. I grabbed her from behind and immediately started doing the Heimlich. I had studied this before, but I had never had to put it into practice. I began doing it so hard I was lifting her off the ground for what seemed like minutes, wondering when this maneuver was going to work.

As I continued to thrust in and up to dislodge whatever she was choking on, my two older daughters were watching this whole thing happen. My eldest, four and a half, had a face of terror, not knowing exactly what was going on, but that mommy was hurt. My newly turned three-year-old was laughing, thinking that daddy was playing a game with mommy as he picked her up repeatedly. It hit me in the moment that if I didn't prevent my wife from choking, our two daughters would watch their mother die in front of them.

After what felt like an eternity, but was more like 12-15 thrusts, my wife began to breathe again. As she did, we both nearly collapsed on the ground, exhausted from this sprint like adrenaline rush. Immediately, I recognized the trauma that was taking place within me. Death is hard for me to handle as it is, but the death of my wife in my hands in front of our daughters would send me over the edge. The reality of that hit me – the true fragility of life, and how it can be lost at any moment.

I was shaking and my thoughts were running away with me, covering all the "what if's" that could have happened. I tried gathering my thoughts for hours, but couldn't seem to shake them. Buster showed up, taunting me that I wasn't prepared enough to protect my family. It was then that I knew I had to find a quiet space, meditate, and have a conversation with myself. That is when Alexander Wolfe showed up and helped to talk me off the ledge. Here's how it went:

*Alex: Man, I'm having a hard time with this. All I can see is Ashley's face as she burst into my office. I see the kids staring at me. Watching me struggle as I do everything that I can to save her.*

*Wolfe: Yeah, but Alex, you did it. You rose to the occasion. You mentally prepare for these things, and you did it.*

*Alex: But I keep running it through my head - what if I didn't? What if my children watched their mother die because I couldn't handle the situation? Now all I can think about is all the other things I'm ill prepared for.*

*Wolfe: You can't think that way. That's not how life works. You know this – you need to focus on the positive. At any moment she could leave, go drop the kids off at school, and not come back. Those things happen all the time. Here, she came back. You know this rule - "feel your shit, acknowledge your shit, but don't lose your shit." It's OK if you talk it out. Feel it. But when you're ready, recognize that she's still here. Be grateful for that.*

*Alex: I am grateful for that. I'm just realizing the true fragility of life in our daily lives. And what if I wasn't home? What if I was off at work, or traveling, or at the gym? What would have happened? My daughters would have watched their mom die right in front of them.*

*Wolfe: The reality is that life is fragile. And those things unfortunately happen all the time. And there's nothing you can do about it. Since they're so far beyond control, let it go. You need to acknowledge what you did, not what you didn't do in an infinite number of hypothetical situations. You know what Seneca said, "We often suffer more from imagination than we do from reality." And right now, your imagination is taking hold. You did not just what you could do, but what anyone could have done. We have to realize that even when you do all that you can, there are going to be things out of your control.*

*Focus on what you're grateful for. In fact, give me five things you're grateful for right now.*

*Alex: I'm grateful for my family, especially knowing what could have happened. I'm grateful for my job. I'm grateful for my health. I'm grateful for my support network, especially at this point. I'm grateful for my mom. I called her and had a conversation with her about what happened, and she listened, and she encouraged, and she supported, and I'm grateful for that.*

*Wolfe: Alright. Breathe this out. Your life is happening right now. Not in the past. Not in the future. It's right now. Go be with your family and be grateful for the time you have with them. It could end at any time. Be the best person you can be in every single moment and live up to the person that everybody knows you can be. You got this.*

Immediately after the conversation with Alexander Wolfe, I felt better. Not back to 100%, but much better than before. I then went and hugged my wife and expressed what I was feeling – this deep sense of vulnerability, fear, and self-doubt. She acknowledged she felt the same way, and we talked about how we can support each other through this and future events like this. Had I not had this conversation with Wolfe, I would not have had a cool enough head to recognize, and then articulate, my feelings emotions. I wouldn't have been able to have the conversation with my wife that made her feel better and acknowledge what she was feeling as well. Buster would have taken over, and I would have gone down my dark hole of negative thoughts. This is how stress and / or trauma affects me, much like how it does everyone. If we can't get ahead of it, it can consume us. Becoming a Subjective Spectator and conversing with ourselves via our Good Wolf is a great way to start that conversation and gain control of your inner dialogue. From there, we can engage our support network to further the support. But the support needs to start from within, and that is what you can achieve through Subjective Spectating and speaking with the best version of you.

---

Learning to use this tool of Subjective Spectating can be massively impactful as we look to overcome past stressors and traumas. It's something I use every time I feel Buster feeding on my past as he tries to knock me off the rails in the present as I aim towards attaining my future. But that is the beautiful thing about Subjective Spectating - it can be used not only for past traumas, but in real time, too.

In the last chapter, we discussed how our thoughts feed off of our attitude and emotions. So, in order to control our thoughts in the heat of the moment, we need a tool to help us keep perspective on our attitude and emotions. Fortunately, studies have been done to help us understand exactly how to do that. "Flies On The Wall Are Less Aggressive[2]" was a study conducted to understand how self-distancing (third-person) compared to self-immersion (first-person) can help control anger in the heat of the moment.

In this study, 94 college students volunteered under the cover story of helping the experimenters understand how different music affected problem solving. The reality of the study was to give the students troublesome problems to solve in a short amount of time while demanding that they be louder and clearer in their responses, all to illicit frustration in the participant. The arduous task that the students were given was to solve 14 large anagrams, i.e. PANDE-MONIUM. Each anagram was to be solved within 7 seconds and then shared back to the proctor, who was part of the experiment.

Upon completing the anagram and sharing their responses, the participants were then repeatedly told that they were not being loud enough by the proctor. This would happen after each time the participant recorded and shared their response to the anagram they were solving. After the fourth anagram was shared, the proctor replied aggressively with, "Look, I can barely hear you. I need you to speak louder, please." After the eighth anagram was shared, the proctor replied impatiently, "Hey, I still need you to speak louder, please!" Finally, after the 12th anagram, the proctor said in a highly frustrated tone, "Look, this is the third time I have to say this! Can't you follow directions? Speak louder!" All of this was done with the purpose of pissing the participant off. I can confidently say that it would have worked on me.

Once they were done solving the anagrams and reporting them, the participants were asked to reflect on the task. They were told that this second task of reflection was to see how music affected creativity and feelings. They instructed the participants to go back and experience this anagram task in their "mind's eye." Some were asked to do this and see themselves from their own eyes as if they were experiencing this again themselves – in a first-person perspective, while some were tasked with viewing this experience as a Subjective Spectator – from a third-party perspective. They did this for 45 seconds and were asked to record their results.

At the end of the 45 seconds of reflection, the participants rated how they experienced the events in their mind on a scale from one to seven. One is what they labeled as "immersed participant", or first-party perspective, where seven was labeled as distanced observer, or what we call Subjective Spectator. From there, they were asked to rate how angry, irritable, hostile, or annoyed they felt based on their perspective. The results were exactly what they were hoping to identify.

After summing up and concluding their calculations as a result of the study, they found that self-distancing, or Subjective Spectating, had a significant impact. As theorized in their hypothesis, those who acted as Subjective Spectators and self-distanced had fewer aggressive thoughts and angry feelings than those who were self-immersed. This first study concluded that you can, in fact, reduce your reactions immediately following a provocation through self-distancing.

Graph one, shared below, illustrates the measurements of anger between those that were "self-immersed" and those that "self-distanced." The measurements were captured by assessing how each participant was feeling "right now", and rated how "angry", "irritable", "hostile", and "annoyed" they felt. Each response was then averaged into the anger index. As illustrated in the graph, those that self-distanced, or used the Subjective Spectating tool, had significantly less anger than those that did not. This clearly outlines the power this tool gives us. It helps us control our thoughts, emotions, and attitude, leading to helping us control the inner narrative and the words we use when speaking to ourselves.

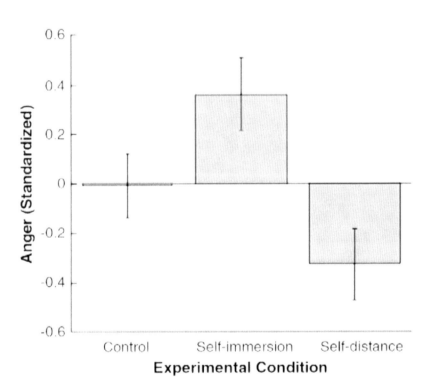

The study continued, aimed at addressing the same hypothesis – can you control your emotions through self-distancing? The second experiment included 86 more college students with varying backgrounds and cultures. This time, the cover story, while similar, was the use of music on creativity and team processes. The participants were told that they would compete with other college students of the same sex, when, in reality, they were tested individually. They introduced a little competition to spice things up…

The first task was the same – solving difficult anagrams under time constraints while listening to music. However, the participants didn't receive a provoking narrative from the proctor, but from their teammate. This, in my opinion, reflects reality better than the first experiment where a proctor was provoking the participants. After all, we are constantly required to work in teams. Can you really use Subjective Spectating in real time to maintain control within your team?

The participants then went head-to-head in competition. They partnered two participants up to compete with their partner on trial reaction time. They were required to respond faster to a visual cue than their partner. The loser received blasts of noise through their headphones. The noise level was pre-selected prior to each head-to-head trial, ranging from level one of 60 dB to level 10 of 150dB. For reference, a casual conversation you may have is around 60 dB. It can impair your hearing around 135 dB. So at 150 Db, which is right around the dB of fireworks going off, you would certainly reach the point of wanting to punch your partner in the throat when they send that sound through your headphones. Maybe that's just me…

Again, the participants were asked to do the same reflective exercise – either take a first or third-party perspective and analyze their emotions during the experiment. From there, they compared the emotional responses.

# THIS TIME, NOT ONLY DID THE FIRST-PERSON GROUP FALL INTO SELF-IMMERSION AND HIGHER LEVELS OF ANGER, BUT SO DID THE CONTROL GROUP, WHICH BEFORE, WAS MINIMALLY AFFECTED. THIS MEANT THAT THOSE THAT DID NOT ACTIVELY PRACTICE A THIRD-PARTY PERSPECTIVE AUTOMATICALLY FELL INTO SELF-IMMERSION, WHICH ULTIMATELY LED TO HIGHER LEVELS OF ANGER.

Conversely and as expected, those who did practice Subjective Spectating displayed lower levels of aggression and anger, as shown in the graph below.

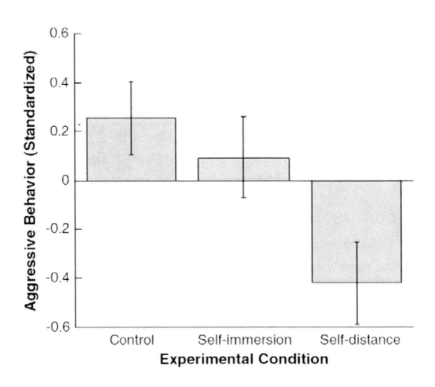

To conclude this study, not only did the experimenters confirm their hypothesis:

# SELF-DISTANCING (SUBJECTIVE SPECTATING) REDUCES AGGRESSIVE BEHAVIORS - BUT THEY ALSO CONFIRMED THEIR PREDICTION THAT MOST PEOPLE NATURALLY ADOPT A SELF-IMMERSED PERSPECTIVE WHEN TRIGGERED. THIS FURTHER HIGHLIGHTS THE NEED TO DEVELOP THIS TOOL.

Not only does it help us when we use it, but naturally we are predisposed to not use it, leading down a darker, less controlled path.

---

"Never let the future disturb you. You will meet it, if you have to, with the same weapons of reason which today arm you against the present," - Marcus Aurelius. As with many things said by thought leaders, it still begs the question of how. How can I not worry about the future? It's much easier said than done. Fortunately, using Subjective Spectating can help with the future just as it can with the past or present.

For our final study, "Self-Talk as a Regulatory Mechanism: How You Do It Matters[3]" walks us through the importance of why taking a non-first person perspective really makes a difference. Each study reviewed touches on why self-distancing is important. It helps us control our thoughts, emotions, words, and even actions. But now we need to answer how we do that. This one further proves one crucial point - that while I'm crazy, I'm justifiably so.

The Self-Talk study comprised six experiments. That being said, we're going to look at two – experiment four and five. To help us understand the outcomes, we first need to understand the language used in the study.

The main thing that the experiment analyzed to assess participants anxiety was the assessment of Challenge vs. Threat. This is something that we will dive into in more detail in the next chapter, so for now, let's focus on the definition of the two. Not to oversimplify, but to explain plainly, our brains assess tasks in two fundamental ways – 1) is this something I can accomplish (Challenge), or 2) is this task too large for me to handle (Threat). When the brain perceives a task to be too large for us to handle, we perceive this task as a threat, leading to stress and anxiety. This kick starts our Sympathetic Nervous System. Our SNS handles our fight, flight, or freeze response and leads to us experiencing increased heart rate, increased breathing rate, sweating, dry mouth, etc. This sums up anxiety. However, if we perceive the task in the future to be something within our wheel house, our brains see this task as a Challenge. We believe we can handle this challenge, and therefore remain cool, calm, and collected. Ultimately, this perspective of a Challenge is how we want to view everything we take on. But to control that perspective takes a toolset to do so.

Experiment four hypothesized that using non-first-person language when appraising a potentially stressful future event would lead the participant to view this future event as a Challenge rather than a Threat. In order to test this theory, they too used college students, 97 of them, to test their anxiety levels of a future event. The chosen event was a speech that had to be given. This wasn't shared in the study, but I believe this task was given because of the finding that 75% of people have a fear of public speaking – a fear that is greater than the fear of death. That and they couldn't threaten to kill them in the study to elicit stress, so public speaking was the next best thing.

Upon entering the lab where the experiment was taking place, the participants were asked how they felt "right now" using a scale of one to seven. One was very negative and seven was very positive. To measure the Threat response, they compared the initial feelings with their feeling after being introduced to the speech task and then asked, "How demanding do you expect the upcoming speech task will be?" The same scale was used – one being not very demanding and seven being extremely demanding. To measure the Challenge response, the experimenters asked, "How well do you think you will cope with the speech task?" They measured this challenge scale from one to five, one being not very well and five being extremely well. Then, they asked a question to judge anticipatory anxiety, or how the participant saw the future task. This question was, "How stressed / anxious do you feel about the upcoming speech task?" They measured this with the scale from one to seven, one being not very stressed / anxious and seven being extremely stressed / anxious. To comprehend the results, note that higher scores showed participants appraised the task of speaking as more of a Challenge than a Threat. AKA – you want a higher score.

After being asked these questions, the participants then wrote their answers in an essay format they called "Stream of Thought Essays." The participants were asked to write a description of their thoughts that followed a reflection period post questions. The experimenters then looked for keywords that reflected first-person or non-first-person perspective throughout the essays. That allowed them to assign scores to each stream of thought essay and compare them.

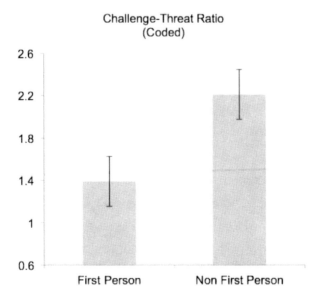

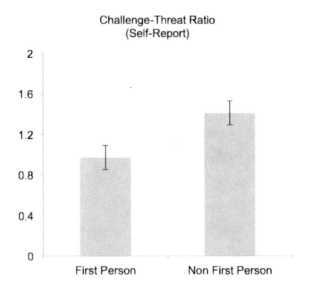

# UPON REVIEWING THESE ESSAYS, THEY FOUND THAT THOSE THAT HAD A NON-FIRST-PERSON PERSPECTIVE – THOSE THAT USED SUBJECTIVE SPECTATING – VIEWED THE SPEECH TASK IN A CHALLENGING WAY RATHER THAN A THREATENING ONE. THEY THEN LOOKED AT THE ANTICIPATORY ANXIETY AND FOUND SIGNIFICANT RESULTS – THOSE WHO USED A NON-FIRST-PERSON PERSPECTIVE REPORTED FEELING LESS ANXIOUS ABOUT THE UPCOMING SPEECH BY NEARLY 50%.

Going back to the Tale of Two Wolves, we took the tactic of Name It to Tame It, but we also took the tactic of Name It to Aim It. We use this aim towards our best self to help us recognize that whatever is placed in front of us is something that we can face head on. As Wolfe would say, "You got this Alex. Look at all you have accomplished before. Why would you think you can't accomplish this, too? I believe in you. You need to believe in you, too. You got this." I know this sounds, and sometimes feels, crazy, but their findings demonstrated that "using non-first-person pronouns and one's own name to refer to the self enhances [Subjective Spectating]." An easy and comfortable way to do that is to imagine yourself in conversation with your best self. What would that person say to you? How would they say it? That is how our self-talk and Subjective Spectating should be approached. Because, as we mentioned before, the relationship you have with yourself is the longest, most raw, most vulnerable relationship you're going to have in your life. You need to make it a good one.

In life, your words matter. In fact, they matter greatly. We express our love through words, poetry, songs, and passionate confession. We also express our anger in explosive verbal jabs that leave unseen wounds for days, months, or years. When it comes to our words, we need to choose them carefully and wisely. This not only needs to be done to those we're speaking to, but more importantly, when we're speaking to ourselves.

The battle of the wolves within is real, and like the Cherokee Chief said, it's happening inside you, me, and all of us. That means that we are not alone in this fight, but to see that, we need to gain a greater perspective, and that is where becoming a Subjective Spectator comes in. As we learn to become this Subjective Spectator, we can increase the space between stimulus and response and remove ourselves from the situation. Whether that is past, present, or future, we can ask the best version of ourselves how he or she would handle what is in front of us. Within this conversation, the Good Wolf will feed us as we feed it, allowing for positive guidance and greater understanding within. From here, we can appraise what is in front of us as a Challenge rather Than a threat, allowing us to take control of the next step in the Mastery Cycle - our actions.

SUBJECTIVE SPECTATOR

TALE OF TWO WOLVES

GOOD WOLF
ALEXANDER WOLFE

EVIL WOLF
BUSTER (REAL ASSHOLE)

NAME TO AIM ⊕

NAME TO TAME

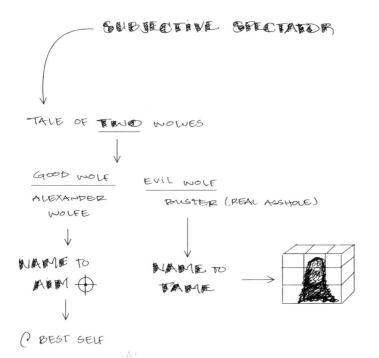

( BEST SELF

⭐ WHEN?

| PAST | PRESENT | FUTURE |
|---|---|---|
| VIEW PAST TRAUMA FROM 3RD PERSON TO FOCUS ON WHAT, NOT WHY | TAKE STEP BACK IN "HEAT OF THE MOMENT" TO REMOVE DEFAULT SELF-IMMERSION DRIVEN BY "ME-JERK" EMOTIONS | USE GOOD WOLF & NAME TO AIM TO HELP VIEW FUTURE AS CHALLENGE & NOT THREAT |

# CHAPTER ACTIVITY
## NAME TO TAME AND AIM

---

Putting theory to practice, the exercise for this chapter is to understand the two wolves within you and name them. You can start with either, but before you just slap a name on it, let's understand who your wolves are.

If you're looking to control your Evil Wolf within, you first need to know what it feeds on that gives it control over you. First and foremost, it feeds on your personal weaknesses, namely self-doubt, insecurities, and personal shame or embarrassment, leading to all the other negative emotions the Cherokee Chief shared with his grandson. For example, if one of your insecurities is that you're a burden to people around you (as mine is) then he will constantly feed on that insecurity and whisper to you, "No one wants you here. They'd all be better off without you." Because of this, we have to become intimately familiar with our own insecurities.

Your Evil Wolf also tries to get you to care more about what others think of you than what you think of yourself. It does this because your trust in yourself and your own capabilities, as we'll discuss in the next chapter, takes away his power. Your Evil Wolf wants you to feel inferior to those around you and get you to worry about what others think of you, their opinion, or your appearance. In reality, none of that really matters. Sure, the perspective of those closest to us matters, as that creates our external reputation, and that is something worth protecting. But the point I'm making is this one shared by Marcus Aurelius:

# "IT NEVER CEASES TO AMAZE ME: WE ALL LOVE OURSELVES MORE THAN OTHER PEOPLE, BUT CARE MORE ABOUT THEIR OPINION THAN OUR OWN."

Your opinion of yourself and belief in yourself needs to matter more than the opinion of everyone else. This is what can take away power from the Evil Wolf. Not only does this allow you to reframe and focus on feeding your Good Wolf, but it starves out the evil one.

Remember, your Evil Wolf tries to break you by isolating you and taking you away from those that care about you. Don't give into that. When you feel the pull to turn inward and away from others, resist it and share with those closest to you what you're thinking. Recall what the Cherokee Chief told his grandson, "This fight is going on within me, you, and EVERYONE." You are never alone in your battle. Don't let your Evil Wolf convince you otherwise.

To get to know yourself on this level, a simple writing exercise can help. Take as much time as you need - 20 minutes should do. Write what you think your Evil Wolf can feed on. What are your insecurities? What worries you and prevents you from acting as you'd wish?

What negativity in your mind hinders you from progress? Be honest with yourself, as you can only fight an enemy as well as you know the enemy. As you write all of this down, associate this with your Evil Wolf - your Buster. This will begin the Subjective Spectator process and will help you be able to see him/her as something within you, but that no longer defines you. You are not your negativity. It's time we controlled that.

The fastest way to control it is to Name It To Tame It. Now that you know what your Evil Wolf feeds on, slap a name on it and tell it to pound sand, go kick rocks, or simply to piss off. Your Buster is no longer in charge. YOU ARE. Name it, tame it, lock him in a cage that only you have a key to.

As we look to put into practice Name It To Aim It, we must first define our Good Wolf as we did our evil one. This practice is fun, as we can get a glimpse into how we define our best lives. As a note, this vision of a "best life" will change over time. Each part of life comes with different goals, but no matter which chapter you're in, there are goals nonetheless.

Using an old Samurai Bushido Code method, we want to focus on death. I know it sounds backwards - to live our best life, we have to think about death - but hear me out. As the Samurai code states:

# "ONE WHO IS SUPPOSED TO BE A WARRIOR CONSIDERS IT HIS FOREMOST CONCERN TO KEEP DEATH IN MIND AT ALL TIMES, EVERY DAY AND EVERY NIGHT...."

*If people comfort their minds with the assumption that they will live a long time, something might happen, because they think they will have forever to do their work and look after their parents, they may fail to perform for their employers and also treat their parents thoughtlessly.*

*But if you realize that the life that is here today is not certain on the morrow, then when you take your orders from your employer, and when you look in on your parents, you will have the sense that this may be the last time - so you cannot fail to become truly attentive to your employer and your parents…*

*In any case, when you forget death and become inattentive, you are not circumspect about things. You may say something offensive to someone and get into an argument. You may challenge something you might as well have ignored, and get into a quarrel….*

*When you always keep death in mind, when you speak and when you reply to what others say, you understand the weight and significance of every word as a warrior by profession, so you do not engage in futile arguments. As a matter of course you do not go to dubious places even if people invite you, so there is no way for you to get into unexpected predicaments. This is why I say you will avoid myriad evils and calamities if you keep death in mind[4]. "*

There is more to this, but the message is clear - as we keep death in mind, we live more fully because we realize how close it always is. That is this exercise.

Going back to the previous chapter, we use a bit of controlled fear to help us discover our potential. I want you to visualize yourself on your deathbed. But rather than be surrounded by all of your loved ones, you're surrounded by all the unfulfilled dreams that you never gave life to. At the foot of your bed is the best version of yourself, standing there with a smile. He or she, being the best version of you, has fulfilled all the things that you only wished you had. And this is where the conversation starts. What does this best version of you tell you as you lie on your deathbed? Here's what mine tells me:

*"Alex, whether you like it or not, your life is one that is supposed to be filled with service to others, focused on helping them overcome themselves in order for them to live their best lives. That means that while others are surrounding you with play, your responsibility and calling is to work. Because of that, you must be very specific with your time and energy management. You and your family are your number one priority. Do not get distracted by flashy people or flashy things around you. If you are to achieve your fullest potential, you must always stay focused on your process of self-mastery, creating, and service to others.*

*That being said, do not get lost in your calling at the expense of your wife and children. They are the source of everything you do. The line between personal greatness and personal detriment, in your case, is a thin one, making it easy to cross. Do not lose yourself in your work to serve others at the cost of losing your family. In your pursuit of serving others, always put the needs of your family unit first. If you don't, that will not only lead to your personal fall, but will be the largest regret you have in life.*

*Always lead by example and let your actions speak for themselves. Be confident, yet minimal in your speaking. Listen more than you speak, for that is where inspiration for service is found.*

*Amongst everything, remember that you are nothing. Whether you are a great, worldwide success, or a small leader within your family, your purpose will be fulfilled, and in the end, you will be buried in the same box and the same dirt. Live a life of love, passion, purpose, and impact. I'm always here if you need to talk."*

The conversation you have with the best version of you is intimately personal and will change from life chapter to life chapter. My conversations with Alexander Wolfe, as I've named him, change from time to time, but in the end, he has the same message. Strive to be your best. I'm here to help you become that every day. Wolfe becomes my own personal philosopher and defender against Buster whenever I need him. Most importantly, he helps me become a Subjective Spectator in nearly every situation. He helps me gain perspective, love more fiercely, and empathize more deeply. Without him, I'd be trapped in a world of my thoughts, and that is often a personal prison.

Take some time to visualize and write your conversation with your best self. Then give him/her a name fitting for your best self. What advice does he/she give you? Analyze that and think about why he/she would give you that advice. Then, make a personal commitment to strive to live that way every day. When you realize that you're not, become a Subjective Spectator to your own life and have the conversation with your best self why you're not. Then go commit to doing it again, and again, and again. You got this, my friend.

# CHAPTER 3
## WHY ME VS. TRY ME
### "ALL SPEECH IS VAIN AND EMPTY UNLESS IT BE ACCOMPANIED BY ACTION." - DEMOSTHENES

---

I was 20, almost 21, and supposed to be at the height of my health, performance, and abilities. At least that's what I thought my 20's would consist of. Fortunately for me, (and we'll address that word later), it wasn't.

I was living in Canada performing service for my church with a bunch of other 20 something-year old dudes. We were having a blast. The summers were hot and humid and the winters were freezing. I mean beyond freezing. Coming from California, I had never truly experienced cold. Canada showed me what cold really meant when it hit -40 degrees and froze my eyelids shut as the steam from my breath crusted my eyelashes together.

What started out to be a fun adventure for my 21-year-old self ended with a twist I wasn't anticipating. I guess if I had anticipated it, it wouldn't have been much of a twist, would it? Anyway, what started out as an experience of service, selflessness, learning, traveling, cultural indoctrination, and life long camaraderie ended in hospital trips, rug burns, and an old dude's fingers up my ass. Needless to say, my reality and my expectations were no longer aligned.

I had always been a sick kid. I was born with asthma and have carried an inhaler with me since I was two. I've always had weird food allergies and saw a "witch doctor" in my early teen years to try to heal me of them. I could be, and still can be, killed by peanuts and shrimp. But none of that has ever stopped me. I played sports throughout my youth. Ice hockey and lacrosse were my jam. I was captain of my teams, made varsity lacrosse my freshman year in high school, and was always looking to be the tough guy with the biggest hits and best fights. I may lose to a peanut, but I was determined to never lose in a competition, no matter how many puffs of my inhaler I had to take. If there was a challenge, I was willing to accept.

That was my outlook until my grandmother died. I've written enough about that so I won't bore you with more details, but that traumatic experience changed my outlook on life. I no longer had this determination to be the best, to put forth effort, to act at all, really. All I wanted to do now was curl up in a ball in the corner and be left alone to die. I guess I could have just eaten a peanut...

This shift in how I perceived life led me down a dark path. Eventually, what was once just some weird allergies turned into some kind of mysterious, yet serious, illness. I lost weight quickly, dropping to 140 - 145lbs my senior year in high school. My energy levels were lower than they had ever been. What was noticeably alarming, however, was my eosinophil count.

For a quick background, eosinophils are part of your white blood cells that consume foreign substances. For example, they "fight substances related to parasitic infection that have been flagged for destruction by your immune system. [They] regulate inflammation. Eosinophils help promote inflammation, which plays a beneficial role in isolating and controlling a disease site." (Mayo Clinic).

A normal eosinophil count is below 500, ideally around 350 or lower, and should be between 0-6% of your blood volume. If you have a count that is higher than 500, which I found out years later that I do - I sit around 1,100 on any given day - then you have what's called "Eosinophilia". When you Google it, you get, "Eosinophilia (e-o-sin-o-FILL-e-uh) is a higher than normal level of eosinophils. Eosinophils are a type of disease-fighting white blood cell. This condition most often indicates a parasitic infection, an allergic reaction or cancer." Fantastic. Thanks Google.

While I now know that I have Eosinophilia, which most likely means that I have Eosinophilic Asthma to go along with my Eosinophilic Esophagitis, (I'm that weird kid at parties that can never eat the snacks or cake and kills the vibe most of the time), I'm fine. I workout 5-6 days a week, eat healthy, and train hard. I've run a marathon (more on that later), done endurance challenges, and I can hold weight on. But this is only as of the last 10-11 years.

Now that you are educated on eosinophils, let's continue... We noticed my eosinophils were high. And we're not talking 1,100 like they are now. Back then, they were up to 1,744, which came out to be 16% of my total blood volume. This most likely indicated cancer - leukemia. My parents, like any good, loving parents would, freaked out, but kept cool heads. We got into a doctor as quickly as we could to dive deeper. The next step was a bone marrow biopsy.

I can still remember this experience like it was yesterday. I went with both of my parents. I was dating my girlfriend - my wife now. I was thinking about all the things I still wanted to do as a kid and realizing that if I had cancer, it would all blow away like dust in the wind.

As we walked into the doctor's office, my dad went with me to get numbed up and ready for the biopsy. I laid down on the table, my dad held my hand, and they stuck a long needle into my lower back. I didn't like how it felt at all, but I was glad it was over. And then I realized that what I had just felt was the numbing agent. They hadn't done the biopsy yet. I was terrified now.

After a few minutes, they came back in with the big needle. The one you could use as a straw or a breathing tube. Again, I was terrified. As my dad continued to hold my hand as they inserted the long needle into the skin and muscle of my back. I couldn't feel much and thought I was in the clear. Then I heard the doctor say, "Okay, you're going to feel some pressure now," as he leaned into me as if we were wrestling over the last piece of gluten-free, dairy free, sugar free cake. He was pushing this straw-like needle on my bone, and we were all waiting for it to pop, which it eventually did. It was actually more of a "crack" as he broke a piece of the bone off. You could hear it and feel it as my body shook from the release of pressure he was putting on me to break through the bone. With a twisting motion, he broke a piece of the bone clean off, removed some marrow, and concluded this part of the biopsy. Now it was time to wait for results.

I don't need to dive into any more details - long story short, the test came back negative, which was a huge positive. I didn't have cancer! We celebrated for a while, and then asked ourselves, "Then what is causing the extremely high eosinophil count?" We didn't find the answer to this question for a few more years.

Eventually, with a year of doing all that we could to make me healthier, I had some semblance of normalcy. Enough to allow me to go on this service adventure for my church. I don't think that I had disclosed this whole "possible cancer" experience, mostly because we didn't have an answer for it. When they asked if I had health conditions that would prevent me from going, I responded "no" because I had none to report. As long as I had my trusty inhaler with me, I was up for anything. Whatever blip I had on my radar seemed to be gone. Or so I thought.

Fast forward to August 25, 2010. It's my 20th birthday and I'm now "reporting for duty" for my service. I couldn't be more excited about going on this adventure. It's the first time I'm leaving the house and venturing out on my own. My expectation is that I'll be the best at this thing that there ever was. But again, life seems to have a funny way of dictating reality over our expectations.

For the sake of expediency, I'm going to bullet point my health journey over my year of service:

- Three weeks into my service I'm in the hospital with 104 degree fever. No one can figure out why.

- Three months into service, when I get to Canada, the people that we're serving are feeding us so much that I throw up after many meals because I can't hold down my food.

- Four or five months into my service, I begin bleeding out of my rear end. I have to wear women's pads while I work so I can hide my bleeding. (Don't you judge me - I got the job done.)

- Seven or eight months in, I finally speak to the local service nurse and she informs me I have to speak to a doctor.

- Nine months in - May 2, 2011, I'm sitting in the hospital with my gown on, finishing my diarrhea from the gallon of laxative I had to take to prepare for my colonoscopy. I remember this date because this was the day that President Obama announced we had killed Osama Bin Laden. I was cheering in the hospital as I contained myself from pooping all over the floor.

- Ten-ish months in, I've got an old dude lubing up his gloved finger to stick it up my rear end to check for fissures to account for the blood - no fissures.

It's around this time that I lose weight - 20 to 25lbs in about two weeks. I had gone from roughly 185lbs to roughly 145lbs. With the loss of weight came the loss of energy, focus, willpower, determination, and zest for life, let alone the service I was attempting.

And we're back to the top - I was about to be 21 and was "supposed to be" at the peak of my health and performance as a young man. With the history of health I had been experiencing while out serving, I didn't think it could get much worse. The good news was that I was still out on this adventure and didn't have to be sent home. That all changed when I blacked out. Twice.

With the quick weight loss I had experienced, my body shut down on me. The first time I passed out, I stood up to get off the couch to go get another bowl of oatmeal - that was the only food that I could eat. BAM! Face plant on the table. My buddy picked me up and helped get me back on the couch. I told him that this would be our little secret, which he kindly agreed to. But then it happened again a few days later. I was getting dressed to go out and get to work when I bent over to pull my pants up. Then the next thing I know I'm coming to, face down on the carpet with my pants around my ankles. My head was throbbing from smashing the floor, and my face felt hot from the rug burn I had gotten on my cheek as I slid forward after hitting the ground. I knew I had to say something.

There was a rule where I served that if you passed out, they would have to medically send you home. They couldn't risk you passing out while out serving and being struck by a vehicle or something. That's why when I blacked out the first time, I knew I couldn't say anything. I wanted to stay out and serve. But when the second one happened, I knew it was going to continue to happen until I somehow fixed whatever was happening with me. True to the rules they had set, they sent me home so that I could return to normal health with the proper resources to help me.

When I got home, it came down to decision time. How was I going to approach my healing process? I was exhausted, my health was in the tank, I had come home early from my service and appeared to be a failure (and I felt like one). We had no real inclination about what was wrong with me. I had been told that they thought I had serious IBS or Crohn's, and fortunately it was early stages and was mild. Unfortunately, though, there was, and still is, no solution to Crohn's. There was medication that can help mask the symptoms, but there was nothing that could fix the root cause of my problems. With all the emotions I was feeling and the hopeless information I was getting, I felt trapped in a lose-lose situation. Quite frankly, I didn't have enough energy to even make a decision like I needed to. Fortunately, I had my mom to help me.

My mom is a Registered Nurse. With her background as a nurse and my loving mother, she knew that there was nothing that the medical community could offer at the time that would help fix the root of my problems. I'll never forget what she did. She looked at me and said something bold and loving along the lines of,

# "ALEX, YOU CAN TAKE THE EASY ROUTE OF MEDICATION AND PUT A BANDAGE ON THIS, OR YOU CAN TAKE THE HARD ROUTE AND TRY TO FIX THIS NATURALLY WITH FOOD. I THINK YOU NEED TO TAKE THE SECOND, FOOD BASED ROUTE, BECAUSE WE NEED TO FIX THIS, NOT MASK IT, BUT THE CHOICE IS UP TO YOU."

I don't know if I chose what I did because my mom told me to or because I actually thought it was the right thing to do, but we went with the natural route and tried to fix my gut and health issues with food. My journey to health had started.

---

I share this story to illustrate how life happens. My expectations, or perception of how life should have been for me, did not match my reality. It's a fool's errand to think that one can change reality to match expectations, so what has to change is you and your perception. You have to realign with reality. Reality will not realign with you. It's the hard truth. Life is going to happen the way it is going to happen, and the only thing you can do is react. But how you perceive life happening is going to determine your actions, for better or worse.

Up to this point, we've discussed the power of your thoughts - ultimately, they become your destiny. They do that by controlling your Mastery Cycle. Following your thoughts are your words. These words don't have to be spoken out loud to others. Often, what we say to others doesn't reflect our inner truth. More importantly is the inner dialogue that we have with ourselves and our two wolves that we've given names to. That inner dialogue, how we speak to ourselves daily and through times of trial, is ultimately going to determine our perception of how life is happening around us. Are we a victim to life or are we capable of facing life head on to become the victor?

From our words - our inner dialogue - comes our actions. These actions will eventually lead to habits, character, and our destiny. Our actions determine the value of our life. If our actions are good, our life is good. If they are bad, our life is bad. It's as simple as that. Intentions matter, sure, but more importantly, are our actual actions taken. After all, the road to hell is paved with good intentions.

To ensure our actions are good, we need to understand how what we perceive leads to what we achieve. How we perceive life, and how we perceive ourselves within life, will determine how we act. This comes down to the tools we have to handle what life places before us. The tools needed will be individual to what you confront, but at the core, we aim all the tools at the same purpose.

# DO WE BELIEVE WE CAN HANDLE WHAT HAS BEEN PLACED IN OUR PATH? OR DO WE BELIEVE THAT THE DEMAND THAT IS NOW ON OUR SHOULDERS IS TOO MUCH FOR US TO BEAR?

This is known as our Challenge vs. Threat Appraisal, and is the outcome of everything we've discussed thus far.

Simply put, our Challenge vs. Threat Appraisal comes down to us feeling that we have the tools or skills to address a task that has been placed before us. If we feel like we have the tools to accomplish this task, we appraise the task as a Challenge. If we think we don't have the tools needed, then we appraise the task as a Threat. Pretty simple. Except it's not.

The natural question following the above statement should be, "Great - what are the tools that I need to view life as a Challenge and how do I get them?" Therein lies the difficulty. Studies have been done repeatedly trying to grasp how we can judge this reaction so that we can control this reaction. Some studies suggest that a Challenge has a different physiological response within the body, keeping the heart rate lower than a Threat response. Other studies suggest that the heart rate doesn't change between Challenge and Threat, but a Threat responses leads to an increase in blood pressure. Some studies suggest that it's not the task that is placed before us, but how we assign a level of importance to this task. Are people watching? Do we view the "failure" of this task as detrimental? Are we concerned about what others are going to think about us based on our performance of this task? Because each person is different, studies seem to vary on how Challenge and Threat present themselves within us. The common thread throughout all of them, however, comes down to how we perceive our capability to handle the task and whether we assign importance to this task. Sound familiar?

Going back to our thoughts and the 12,000 to 60,000 thoughts we have per day. Are we controlling them or are they controlling us? Our thoughts are evolutionarily more negative, so are we perceiving life to be more negative, or are we adjusting our perspective to see life through a more positive lens? How are our words, especially to ourselves? Do they reflect victimhood? "Why would this happen to me? Why does it always have to be me? Why did it have to happen like this?" Or are we speaking to ourselves in a way that allows us to maintain control and therefore become the victor? "Alex, you got this. You've handled other things like this before - if you could conquer those things, you can conquer this. Get to work!" And now, how are our actions reflecting your thoughts and inner dialogue?

The foundational tools that are needed to view life and its demands as Challenges over Threats are all internal ones. We can break them down into three main points:

# CONFIDENCE IN OURSELVES
# CONNECTION TO OUR GOALS AND HIGHER SELVES
# CONTROL WHAT WE CAN CONTROL

First, confidence in ourselves. In psychology, confidence in self, or self-efficacy, is our belief in our own capacity to act in the ways necessary to reach specific goals. The etymology of confidence is *con fidere*, being of latin origin. Con, meaning with, fidere, meaning to have full trust or reliance. So if we need to develop the tool of SELF-confidence, we need to develop full trust or reliance with OURSELVES. This is the first tool used in acting towards our desired outcomes or goals. But how do we develop full trust or reliance within ourselves? That's a fantastic question.

To avoid making this too difficult, let's ask a different question before we answer the one just asked. How do you develop trust in others? I want you to think about someone that you trust deeply, someone you can fully rely on. How did you get to that point with them? Think about that - I'll wait... Aaaaaaaaand we're back. Who'd you think of and why? I'd suggest you write how you came to trust them so you can learn from their wonderful example. The person who came to my mind is my best friend, Braden.

Braden and I have been friends since high school. It started out as a group of friends, but he and I clicked when I got sick - he was always there. He was there for me when I was on my liquid diet and while I was vegan. He even ate some things that I had to eat to support me. When I added chicken back into my diet for the first time via a taco, he was there to partake in my happiness. He and I became gym partners and during our workouts, he never once quit on me. No matter how tired he was, he stuck it out. He would say, "Man it's been a long day, I'm exhausted." To which I replied with sincerity, "No worries man. If you need to go, you can. I'll finish myself and catch up with you later." His response was a glare into my soul, followed by, "If you're still going, I'm still going. I'll never quit on you." That statement, while outstanding in the gym, was even cooler in real life, and he meant it. I've changed workout partners on him and left him (I have since repented for my sins). I've changed careers, moved across different states, gotten married, had kids, and he has always been there for me. I'm an introvert who goes to bed at 8:00pm, wakes up at 4:00am, doesn't have much of a social life, eats weird, and enjoys suffering - I'm really not a fun friend to have. Nevertheless, Braden has been there through everything and has never once even had the thought of leaving. On top of all of that, when he says he's going to do something, he does it. Zero questions. So I know that If I ask him for some help and he commits to it, I can rely on him 100%. Along with that, he's not going to tell me he can do something if he can't do it. He won't make any promises he knows he can't keep. With all of this, I have come to trust Braden with my life. He is the perfect example of how to gain trust in others, and also the perfect example of how we can develop confidence in ourselves.

The pattern that Braden developed with me is one of deep confidence in him. He is loyal to me. He keeps his promises and doesn't negotiate after he makes a commitment. He won't commit to something he can't honor or live up to. He supports me in my dark times, and he is there to celebrate with me during the great times. He wants the best for me, but doesn't coddle me. If I need to pull myself together, he calls me on it with love. He never leaves me carrying weight he knows I can't handle - he's always there to help lighten the load. And in the end, he loves me as a brother, no matter what. I can FUBAR something, and he'll be there to laugh and point fingers at me, and then he'll help me clean up the royal mess that I made. He has faith in me that no matter how low I get, I'll eventually get back up and be better than before, especially because I have his help. These things are things we need to do for, and with, ourselves.

When it comes to making and keeping promises to yourself, are you one to negotiate with yourself and let yourself slide on your process and performance? If you commit to do something, do you let yourself push it off until it's just too much to deal with? When you need to get your mind right and get back in the game of life, do you coddle yourself and roll in self-pity as the victim? Or can you talk yourself into getting back in the game to become the victor? When times are dark, are you there for yourself to realize that this is just a chapter and that this, too, shall pass? Do you believe you can achieve whatever you set your mind to? Are you loyal to yourself, putting your needs above others to ensure you take care of yourself? Do you want the best for yourself, and do you live up to what you know is best for you? If you can answer these questions as, "Hell yeah!" then I bet you've got great self-confidence. But if you can't, you've got to put in the work to get there. This is not something you'll ever fully attain and get to stop working on. It's a lifelong journey, so start where you are and get moving.

# THE BEST WAY TO GAIN CONFIDENCE IN YOURSELF IS TO COMMIT YOURSELF TO SOMETHING AND FOLLOW THROUGH WITH THAT - NO IF, ANDS, OR BUTS ABOUT IT. YOU NEED TO START MAKING DEALS WITH YOURSELF AND HONORING THOSE DEALS.

If you tell yourself that you're going to do 100 push-ups when you wake up, you better do those right when you wake up. If you don't, you start the day by breaking the promise you made to yourself. If your friends constantly broke the promises they made with you, would you have full trust in them? Then how do you expect to gain full trust in yourself if you don't keep the promises you make to you? You need to start by setting short-term, realistic targets that you can achieve daily. After a while, you begin to understand how to keep the promises you make to yourself. You also come to understand what you can deliver in that moment. Like Braden, don't commit to things you can't honor. If you've never done more than 10 push-ups, then don't commit to 100 daily. Commit to 10 daily for a week. Then commit to 15 daily for a week. Then add other things to that commitment. A good mental start point is this:

# DON'T COMMIT TO WHAT YOU CAN DO ON YOUR BEST DAY, COMMIT TO WHAT YOU CAN DO ON YOUR WORST DAY, AND THEN DO THAT EVERYDAY.

STRONGER THAN YOUR PAIN

To gain this trust in yourself, you have to honor your own commitments, remove any obstacles that can keep you from achieving them, and be consistent. The best way to do that is to start with targets that are too small to fail and that align with what you're connected to.

This is the case because CONFIDENCE needs EVIDENCE. That evidence comes from you doing what you say you will do. We know words are powerful, but words without action are empty. Evidence is you taking action towards your targets, not talking about taking action towards your targets. And those actions need to be to the absolute best of your abilities. We do not do them to the best of someone else's abilities or standards, but to ours.

Self-confidence being derived from effort embodies the, "A for Effort" approach. Unlike school or work reviews, life doesn't give grades or pay raises based on performance, but life does reward you based on your efforts. Call it karma, call it whatever you want, but life has a way (sometimes wrapped in sick humor) of giving back to us what we put out into the world. And what's the number one thing we can put out into the world? Our effort.

John Wooden, considered to be the greatest NCAA basketball coach of all time, would often say:

# "HAPPINESS IS IN MANY THINGS. IT'S IN LOVE, IT'S IN SHARING, BUT MOST OF ALL, IT'S IN BEING AT PEACE WITH YOURSELF KNOWING THAT YOU ARE MAKING THE EFFORT, THE FULL EFFORT, TO DO WHAT IS RIGHT."

Happiness comes from the full effort of doing what is right. If we're always doing our best to do what is right, we can have confidence in ourselves that we achieved what was meant to be achieved. And I know what you're thinking, "But what if my effort to do what was right wasn't good enough?" My rebuttal to that is twofold - 1) Good enough to whom? If your effort was truly your full effort, it should be good enough for you. Forget about what others think - we're building SELF confidence. If your effort was truly your full effort, then you should be happy, or at least accepting of the outcome, because you gave it your all. 2) Life doesn't always give you what you want, but it always gives you what you need. If your effort was your full effort, but that wasn't good enough to get the job or win the game, then life gave you want you needed - a lesson to be better next time. Just because you "failed" at achieving something doesn't mean you are a failure. It simply means you need to do better next time. But if you gave it your all, then you can be proud of your effort. That then feeds your confidence, knowing you did all you could, which leads to the action of further practice to get better. This ultimately leads to winning in the end. Churchill said, "Success is going from failure to failure without any loss of enthusiasm."

# TO DO THAT, WE MUST HAVE CONFIDENCE, EXTREME TRUST, IN OURSELVES REGARDLESS OF THE OUTCOME. THE ONLY WAY TO DO THAT IS TO BASE OUR CONFIDENCE ON OUR EFFORTS, AND THAT EFFORT HAS TO ALWAYS BE EVERYTHING WE HAVE.

The second tool is goal setting and knowing how to CONNECT to your goals and your best self. Not only does goal setting, which if properly done leads to goal achieving, feed our first tool of self-confidence, but it also helps us perceive the demands in life as more of a Challenge than a Threat, leading to greater success. Breaking that run on sentence down - how you set goals matters. You need to connect with your goal on a personal level and know why you are aiming for it. This needs to be a personal decision, an individual choice, not one created through outside influence.

In addition to your goal being achievable, it has to be personal because it has to be backed by a personal "why." Why are you aiming for this goal? If you're looking to achieve something because you want to impress someone, want to make someone else happy, are seeking fame or external validation, you will ultimately fail in the long run. In the short run, you will most likely view this goal as a Threat, leading to a lower probability of success. Studies have shown that how we set our goals matters, and the biggest factor is setting the goal towards personal growth, not achieving results based on performance. Ultimately, our goals should be based on learning, growing, and becoming better than we were before the goal was set and achieved. In this model of goal setting, there is no failure unless you quit, and that, my friend, is the secret to success.

A study done on Olympic athletes - "Psychological Resilience in Olympic Champions[5]" - set out to discover why some athletes win gold whereas others do not. Specifically, they were studying the mindset of these athletes and how they appraise demands in life - as Challenges or Threats - and which tools they used to overcome trials. On goal setting, they discovered that gold medal athletes:

# "WERE ABLE TO FOCUS ON THEMSELVES, NOT BE DISTRACTED BY OTHERS, FOCUS ON THE *PROCESS RATHER THAN THE OUTCOME* OF EVENTS, AND WERE ABLE TO SWITCH THEIR SPORT FOCUS ON AND OFF TO SUIT THE DEMANDS THEY FACED."

These athletes were not focused on beating everyone in the competition - that is far too much pressure to carry while seeking optimal performance. Instead, they focused on what they could control - performing to achieve their personal best. If they performed to their personal best, the outcome would determine itself. If that outcome was gold, fantastic. If it wasn't, fantastic. Because they performed to their fullest capability, and they know they cannot ask more of themselves. This is the mindset needed for consistency, confidence, and longevity of goal setting and achievement. The study concluded with this:

# "THE PARTICIPANTS IN THIS STUDY DESCRIBED OPTIMAL SPORT PERFORMANCE AS FULFILLING THEIR ATHLETIC POTENTIAL RATHER THAN BECOMING AN OLYMPIC CHAMPION."

If the goal of some of the most elite performers in the world is to be THEIR best, not THE best, shouldn't we aim to do the same?

We refer to this type of goal setting as CONNECTION over PERFECTION. The goal that you set should be one that is connected to the best version of you, your inner Good Wolf, not one that drives you towards unattainable perfection set by society around you. We discussed creating the best version of you. What does this best version of you look like, sound like, listen like, perform like, etc? What goals can you create that lead you to becoming that best version of yourself? Those are the goals you need to set, and more importantly, those are the goals you need to honor and make non-negotiable with yourself. When done correctly, setting goals leads to attaining goals, which leads to the development of greater CONFIDENCE in ourselves.

Connecting with our best self, which will always be our future self, is extremely important for proper goal setting. A study by Walter Mischel was done to see how this affected the brain[6].

In his study, his participants entered an fMRI machine - a machine that uses magnetic fields to detect brain activity. He then asked them to view themselves in the present to see which part of the brain lit up. Consistently, the self-center of the brain lit up when participants looked at themselves in the present. Then, Mitchell asked them to think of someone else, leading to the stranger center of the brain lighting up. Following that, he asked them to look ahead and see themselves in the future. What he found was astonishing. As some people looked towards the future, their self-center of the brain continued to light up. But as others looked to the future, the view of the "themselves" lit up their stranger-center of the brain. This indicated that as we look to the future, our ability to align with our goals has to be connected to aligning with our future selves.

# ONE OF THE BIGGEST REASONS WE GIVE UP ON OUR GOALS IS OUR PRESENT SELF CAN'T CONNECT WITH THE FUTURE SELF. WE CAN'T CONNECT THAT THE SACRIFICE IT TAKES NOW IS WORTH WHAT IT TAKES TO ACHIEVE THE GOAL WE DESIRE IN THE FUTURE.

However, if we can bring the future self into the picture more clearly and closer to our present self, the sacrifices needed to achieve our goal become less cumbersome. This is because we realize we will have the gains in the future and not a stranger. Therefore, the exercise of Name It To Aim It is crucial to not only realizing who we want to become, but creating a walkable path to achieve that goal.

The third step to viewing life as a Challenge rather than a Threat to get us to act is CONTROL. There are many aspects to control. Control of the situation, of people in your life (rather than them controlling you), control of time (autonomy) - but most important is control of self. If we can't gain control of ourselves, then nearly every situation that is presented to us is going to trigger a Threat response. Again, with enough effort and training, we can control our thoughts, the emotions that we assign to them, and therefore, the actions that follow our chosen and controlled response. Truth be told, control of self is really the only control that we have in this world. You cannot truly control any situation you're in - there are too many factors outside of your influence. You cannot truly control people because, well, they're people and free to choose on their own. You cannot truly control time - you never know when yours is up. All you can control is yourself - how you act and how you react.

If we have control of ourselves, we can choose how we perceive what is happening to us. We get to choose if the demands put on us are a Threat or a Challenge. In the same Olympic study mentioned above, they found that the most successful athletes could reflect on what had happened to them and then choose how they wanted to react to it, ultimately using the events as motivation for further success:

# "...AN ATHLETE MAY INITIALLY APPRAISE A STRESSOR IN A NEGATIVE MANNER, BUT FURTHER EVALUATES THE RESULTANT EMOTION AS HAVING THE POTENTIAL TO FACILITATE PERFORMANCE, AND THEREBY MAINTAIN RESILIENCE IN STRESSFUL SITUATIONS."

The only way that they can do this is through the tools we've discussed. Controlling your thoughts, viewing yourself and the event that happened as a Subjective Spectator, and then deciding for yourself how you are going to act based on your CONFIDENCE within, your CONNECTION to your goals, and your CONTROL of what is controllable.

## CONFIDENCE

CONFIDENCE NEEDS EVIDENCE. THIS EVIDENCE IS YOU DOING WHAT YOU SAY YOU'LL DO. YOUR COMMITMENTS TO SELF NEED TO BE NON-NEGOTIABLE. NEVER BREAK A PROMISE TO SELF.

## LIFE AS A CHALLENGE

ACT

## CONTROL

YOU NEED TO AIM TO CONTROL WHAT YOU CAN & LET GO OF WHAT YOU CAN'T. WHAT CAN YOU CONTROL? YOURSELF. WHAT CAN'T YOU CONTROL? EVERYTHING ELSE. CONTROL YOUR COMMITMENT TO SELF, YOUR CONNECTION TO YOUR GOALS, & ULTIMATELY YOUR CONFIDENCE IN YOURSELF.

## CONNECTION

YOU NEED TO CONNECT TO YOUR GOALS ON A PERSONAL LEVEL. WHY ARE YOU AIMING AT THIS GOAL? IT SHOULD BE INTRINSIC & RELATED TO PERSONAL GROWTH TOWARDS YOUR BEST SELF.

Now, these tools are great, but we all know that they are much easier said than done. The time that it takes to build confidence in ourselves is a long road. The ability to align our goals and higher selves with a purpose rather than a material thing takes a lot of reflection. The ability to learn to control what we can and let go of what we can't takes a lot of patience and is an endless journey. I get it. But it's possible. People do it every day. And again, that is the key. These tools don't develop and then remain developed - there is no end to this journey, and that's a good thing! You constantly get to work on yourself, to be under construction, to improve and grow daily. That, in and of itself, is a worthy goal, and should be one we all seek after.

Along this journey of learning to develop these tools and skills, you're going to falter. That's life. We all falter from time to time.

## BUT WHEN THAT TIME COMES, RATHER THAN DOUBT YOURSELF AND YOUR CAPABILITIES, DOUBT YOUR DOUBTS.

This is absolutely something that is within our control. When you think, "am I really capable of achieving what I've sought to achieve?", rather than give in to that doubt of self, keep the doubt, but turn it on its head. Doubt your doubts and ask yourself, "Why would I think I'm not capable of achieving my goals? Other than myself, what can truly stop me from getting what I've set out to achieve? Why do I think I'm not worthy of greatness?" Not only does this spin the doubt on its head and reframe towards a positive thought process, it helps you gain control of your Evil Wolf, who eventually and inevitably preys on and controls the negative thought process. When that happens, doubt your doubts, and then act right away.

Many of us think that because we don't feel like doing something, we shouldn't do it. "I don't want to go to the gym. I'm too tired today." "I don't want to sit down and write my book, I'm a terrible writer who has no idea what he's doing." (That's me every morning at 0430). But what we fail to recognize is that not only does our psychology beget our physiology, AKA our mindset determines our actions, but our PHYSIOLOGY BEGETS OUR PSYCHOLOGY, AKA our actions determine our mindset.

In "The How of Happiness[7]" by Sonja Lyubomirsky, Sonja shares a study that compared how exercise (action) compared to taking Zoloft to help mitigate symptoms of depression. The study took two groups and had one group exercise, while the other continued to take Zoloft. What the study found was that exercise was just as effective as taking Zoloft when addressing the symptoms of depression, but more importantly, the positive effects of exercise lasted longer and had almost zero crash. This highlights the PHYSIOLOGY begets our PSYCHOLOGY. When we act, when we move, when we make progress towards our targets and goals, our psychology improves. We don't have to "be in the mood" to act, we need to act to get in the mood. That came out wrong. Or did it?

Sonja further explains that we can break our happiness in life into three pieces, each having a percentage of our happiness. The first variable in the happiness equation is genetic. Our genetics are responsible for 50% of our happiness. For me, I am not naturally as happy as some people I know, which is why these tools we're discussing are so important for me. The second variable is external motivators. Circumstantial motivators account for 10% of our happiness. Here's the big one:

# 40% OF OUR HAPPINESS IS DERIVED FROM WITHIN. THIS INCLUDES OUR ATTITUDE (CHAPTER 1), OUR OUTLOOK OR PERSPECTIVE, AND OUR BEHAVIOR (CHAPTER 2 AND 3).

Our attitude (thoughts and feelings), what we perceive, and what we do (our efforts) accounts for 40% of our happiness, and is all within our control. This is extremely important, because when we are happy, we view life as a Challenge, and when we view life as a Challenge, we are happy. How do we do both things? We focus on controlling what we can control. We've officially come full circle.

When we act in the face of our doubt, we 1) keep the commitment we made to ourselves and show our CONFIDENCE the evidence it needs to grow, 2) we change our mindset to one driven towards success via the process, which is how our GOALS should be made in the first place, and 3) we CONTROL what is controllable. We hit all three of the primary tools needed to view life and its demands as a Challenge rather than a Threat. "I don't want to go to the gym because I'm too tired," turns into "I know that every time I go to the gym I feel better and I have more energy - let's go!" "I don't want to sit down and write my book, I'm a terrible writer who has no idea what he's doing," becomes "I don't care if I'm a terrible writer now, I told myself I would do this. I'll get better as I go, but avoiding the process of writing will not get the book done or make me a better writer. Let's go!" This is literally the conversation I have with myself every morning as I sit down to write. Over time, the conversation gets shorter and shorter. With each day of action comes greater confidence in my capabilities and greater trust in myself. And I've settled that this being my first book, it's probably going to be extremely difficult and time consuming. But my goal is to write it anyway, because I know there is at least one person out there that it's going to help, and that's the goal. I can live with that.

---

Action is, by far, the hardest thing to do, especially to do right. It's easy to do things, but it's hard to do things correctly. Your thoughts are your own, your inner dialogue is private, your words can be rephrased, but your actions speak far louder than your words and they are hard to redo once they are done. You can't un-punch someone, you can't un-crash that car, you can't undo that drug, you can't uncut that wound. With our actions having greater impact on more than just our own lives, their importance is great when it comes to our success in life. That is why our actions, which lead to habit, determine our character, which decides our destiny.

CONTROL → YOU & YOUR ACTIONS

• HAPPINESS is MORE READILY FOUND WHEN WE SEE LIFE AS A CHALLENGE → WE HAVE TOOLS TO HANDLE LIFES DEMANDS

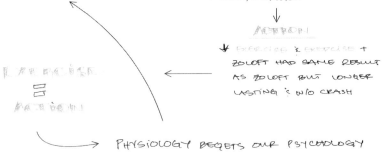

ATTITUDE, OUTLOOK, BEHAVIOR

ZOLOFT HAD SAME RESULT AS ZOLOFT BUT LONGER LASTING & N/O CRASH

→ PHYSIOLOGY BEGETS OUR PSYCHOLOGY

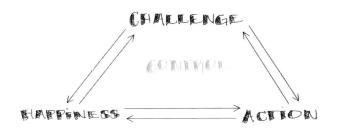

CHALLENGE

HAPPINESS — ACTION

Are your actions driving you towards your desired destiny? Are they an accurate representation of who you want to be? Are they within your control? Or are they simply a result of uncontrolled thoughts and emotions - knee-jerk reactions determined by those people and things around you?

# YOU NEED TO BE THE ONE IN CONTROL OF YOUR ACTIONS, BASED ON THE GOALS YOU SET, AIMED AT BEING THE BEST VERSION OF YOU THAT YOU CAN BE, DAY AFTER DAY AFTER DAY. LIFE'S CHALLENGE HAS BEEN EXTENDED. ARE YOU READY TO ACCEPT IT?

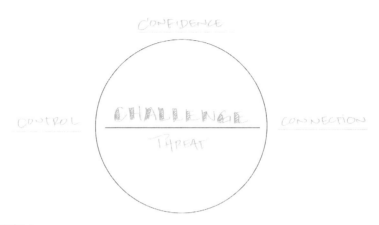

CHALLENGE → HAPPINESS = REALITY - EXPECTATIONS

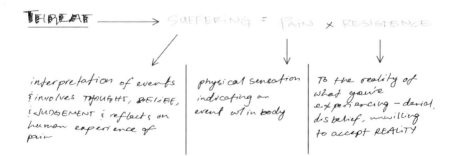

LIFE → HAPPENS W/O OUR CONTROL - MUST ACCEPT

CONTROLLABLE → EMOTIONS, ACTIONS, EXPECTATIONS, RESIST

THREAT → SUFFERING = PAIN × RESISTENCE

| interpretation of events | physical sensation | To the reality of |
| & involves THOUGHT, BELIEF, | indicating an | what you're |
| & JUDGEMENT & reflects on | event w/in body | experiencing — denial, |
| human experience of | | disbelief, unwilling |
| pain | | to accept REALITY |

To finish the journey of my health, I decided to take the natural approach via food. My parents hired a Ph.D in Nutrition to come and work with me at home. She gave me her diagnosis, which was Crohn's, and we treated my health as such, seeking to cure me at the root. She laid out her process that she wanted me to follow and met with me on a weekly basis to support me. We also hired a chef that would come and help us cook meals based on the nutritional guidance that my nutritionist had provided.

For the first six-ish months, I was on a strict liquid diet of soups and green smoothies. I did this so that my gut would have the energy it needed to heal. As my calories were liquid, less digestive effort was needed from my stomach and intestines, leaving them more energy to focus on healing. At least that was the theory. From there, I added in solids, but remained a vegan to avoid any hard to digest foods such as animal fats. To this day, fats are my largest trigger to my flair ups. If I have more than 100g of fat in a day, I know that I'm going to feel sick. But now that I was having solids, I would have salads with some olive oil dressing for more calories, a lot of steamed vegetables as those are easier to digest (I still avoid raw veggies), and fruit that was more easily digestible such as berries. I was a vegan for an additional six months, totaling about a year living the vegan lifestyle.

This approach allowed my gut to heal itself, and after about a year of living this process to the best of my abilities, I decided it was time to add in animal products. This decision was made because while I felt better, I didn't like how I looked and I was still low on energy. I needed more calories. I was still extremely skinny and lacked muscle, which was the opposite of how I wanted to look - how I saw myself within. I added in chicken, fish, and eggs as my principal sources of protein, and remained that way for 10 years. My consumption comprised chicken, eggs (mainly egg whites due to my sensitivity to fat), fish, steamed veggies, white rice, and the occasional fruits. What this really meant - I was dairy free, gluten-free, raw veggie free, raw fruit free, legume free, nut free, red meat free, pork free, and often, flavor free. But at this point I had to decide - did I want to live a life that I controlled? Or did I want to live a life that controlled me? Life was now a Challenge, and one that I could accept. And I still decide to accept it every single day.

I'm still extremely disciplined in my consumption. I'm still dairy free, gluten-free, raw veggie free, legume free, and nut free (except for pistachios). My red meat and pork consumption is minimal. I have cut out all grains except for white rice due to the inflammation that many grains cause me. I don't drink alcohol. I don't take any medications for my gut other than probiotics - my food is my medicine. The challenge has been extended, and I have welcomed it with open arms.

I said at the beginning of this chapter that I am fortunate for these trials. Why? Because over time, they taught me how to view them as Challenges, and that I can do whatever I set my mind to. Mind you, I still have flair ups to this day. If I'm not extremely disciplined, I can be under for a week or more. I ran a marathon and had a flair up at mile 23 (more on that later). Challenge accepted. If I eat apple sauce before I have other foods, I can be in bed for three hours due to the stomach pain. Life is tough, but at least it's not a trial that will defeat me. It's a Challenge, and one that I rise to every morning when I get out of bed at 04:00. Why 04:00? Because that is the hour that I would always have my flair ups. This time used to control me, now I control it. Now it's my time to wake up and conquer the day. Challenge accepted.

Life is always going to throw things your way, but it's within your power to perceive them as Threats or Challenges. The more tools that you develop to control yourself, the better chance you have at perceiving Challenges over Threats, and therefore, the better chance you have at successfully attaining your goals. Not to be cheesy or cliché, but life doesn't get easier, you just get stronger. But becoming stronger is a choice that you have to make every day. Act on it, moment to moment to moment. What you perceive is what you achieve. Perceive that you can do it and you can. Now go get it.

# CHAPTER ACTIVITY
## 100 QUESTIONS

---

The activity for this chapter is aimed to add on to the previous activity. Chapter two's activity was "Name To Tame And Aim" - naming your two wolves within. This chapter's activity is now to work with the best version of yourself to define a goal that you can connect to and seek after. The outcome of this goal setting activity is to have you gain CONFIDENCE in yourself, CONNECT to something that matters to you, along with your best self, and to learn to CONTROL yourself as you push yourself towards success. All three major tools needed to perceive life as a Challenge rather than Threat.

To do this, find some time to sit down with yourself - 30 to 45 minutes - and reflect on what's important to you. I've found that the best way to do this is to have a pen and paper with you, and do an exercise created by Michael Gelb in his book, "How to Think Like Leonardo da Vinci[8]." I mean, who doesn't want to learn how to think like one of the greatest minds in history? With pen and paper in hand, start writing 100 questions. There doesn't have to be a direction at first. As you write more and more questions, eventually a pattern will emerge. Once you have your 100 questions written, notice what themes develop, and then work on selecting your top 10 questions. Put stars next to each question that resonates with you, even if it's more than 10 to start. Then whittle your way down until you have your top 10 questions that reflect what is, at this time, most important to you. From there, you can set a goal around what you have thought of and define a way to get there.

After you've selected your top 10 questions and set your goal, place it where you can see it every day as a reminder of what you're working toward. Give yourself a timeline to achieve this - 30, 60, 90 days, and then go after it with zero negotiations. And by that, I don't mean continue towards this goal if you find that 20 days into it it's no longer important. Suppose your top 10 questions are about how to get into better shape, so you decide to run every day. Twenty days into it, you find you don't enjoy running, so you're thinking of quitting. Sure, quit the running, because that's not the true goal. The true goal is to get into better shape, so reframe your process into something else that will get you there. Go to the gym every day and lift weights. Start jump roping for 30 mins. Ride a bike instead of run. Be non-negotiable with the outcome, but flexible with your means. Focus on the process and stay consistent.

We can use this exercise of 100 questions over and over. Once you've achieved one goal, do the exercise again to see what else comes to the surface of your mind and set a goal to achieve that. The process of goal setting, striving to reach beyond our capabilities, and become better through the journey, is never ending. Learn to love it and you will tap into one of life's greatest secrets to happiness.

Here are my top 10 questions to the 100 Questions Exercise as of 3.3.2023. These are now something I can look at every day and ponder. My goal to achieve, or answer, these questions is to meditate on them daily until I have come to an answer that I can articulate simply. What I will track to achieve this goal is that daily meditation, which will be for a minimum of 10 minutes. I will keep a notebook beside me so that as I receive answers to these questions, I can jot them down. I will carry this notebook with me throughout the day as well, as inspiration strikes at any time. I will then take those notes and review them on a weekly basis - every Sunday - to see the answers that I am getting through the week. I don't know what the timeline will be to get answers to these questions, but I will continue to work towards these goals until I achieved them. Personally, I would like to receive answers to these questions via my meditation within 90 days. That is my targeted timeline that I think is realistic. As I focus on my process, the outcome will produce itself. If I don't have answers by the end of 90 days, I will see which questions remain unanswered and reassess my plan to hit my target. Challenge extended. Challenge accepted. Time to get movin'.

# 100 QUESTIONS : TOP 10

1) WHY DOES OUR LIFE NEED THE APPROVAL OF OTHERS? IF A TREE FALLS W/O SOMEONE THERE TO HEAR IT, DOES IT MAKE A SOUND? IF A LIFE IS LIVED W/ NO ONE THERE TO WITNESS IT, DOES IT HAVE MEANING?

2) IS BEING & BECOMING THE SAME THING SINCE LIFE DOES NOT EXIST IN A VACUUM W/O TIME?

3) DOES SEEKING AFTER THE BEST VERSION OF OURSELVES NOT PUT US ON THE STRAIGHT & NARROW PATH?

4) WHAT IS THE CLIMBING ORDER OF LIFE'S MOUNTAINS — MENTAL, SPIRITUAL, EMOTIONAL, PHYSICAL?

5) IF GOD IS FOUND ATOP MOUNTAINS, DOES CLIMBING LIFE'S MOUNTAINS TOWARD SELF MASTERY NOT BRING US FACE TO FACE W/ HIM?

6) WHICH IS MORE IMPORTANT, LEARNING FROM OUR PAST OR GOALING TOWARDS OUR FUTURE?

7) HOW CAN SOMEONE LIVE A PURPOSEFUL LIFE W/O HAVING A PURPOSE TO FILL IT?

8) IF THE OUTCOME IS NEVER TRULY W/IN OUR CONTROL, HOW DO WE ASSIGN OUR ACTIONS TO ACHIEVE IT?

9) WHAT IS THE EQUATION TO LIVING A SUCCESSFUL LIFE?

10) HOW CAN FAILING AT WHO WE'RE SUPPOSED TO BE DIRECT US TOWARDS BECOMING WHO WE'RE MEANT TO BE?

# SECTION 1 SNAPSHOT
## PUTTING IT ALL TOGETHER

# MASTERY CYCLE

Destiny → Thoughts → Words → Actions → Habits → Character → (back to YOU) with YOU in center

- Thoughts:
  - up to 60 k / day → 80% neg!
  - have no power themselves – get power from emotions
  - life happens → thought occurs → emotion assigned → reaction
  - create space b/w stimulus & response

STIMULUS ← CONTROL → RESPONSE

↓

ATTITUDE:
"Settled way of thinking or feeling."

↓

A T T I T U D E
1  20  20  9  20  21  4  5
= 100%

⎿ MAINTAINED THROUGH ATTITUDE

↓ ↓ ↓

- Words: must reflect thoughts & mirror your attitude

mirror

↓

## SUBJECTIVE SPECTATOR

Tale of Two Wolves

Good Wolf            Evil Wolf
   ↓                    ↓
NAME TO AIM ⊕        NAME TO TAME → Buster
   @
Best Self → A. Wolfe

## WHEN

"PAST ←————————————→ FUTURE

- 3ᴿᴰ Person Perspective
- Remove self from "heat of moment"
- Aim @ Good wolf to determine actions

# CHAPTER 4
## FAIL AT WHO YOU'RE SUPPOSED TO BE

### "THE WORLD WILL ASK YOU WHO YOU ARE, AND IF YOU DO NOT KNOW, THE WORLD WILL TELL YOU."
### - CARL JUNG

---

Who are you? Who do you want to be? How do you become that? It's exceedingly difficult when everyone around you thinks you should be their version of you. Your parents want you to be someone successful by their definition. Your friends need you to be someone supportive, based on their needs. Social media demands that you be someone that fits within their definition of sexy and outlandish. The news expects you to be someone based on their viewing ratings. How can you be all of those things? All of this is weight on your shoulders that keeps you from being your authentic self. To ourselves, though, underneath all the pressure of these suppositions provided by the world, we have an image of ourselves that we want to make a reality. We want to break free of the chains the world has put on us and become who we actually want to be. We want to leave behind the life of the unachievable expectations and start living as the individual that WE see ourselves becoming. But in order to do this, we first have to fail - we have to fail at who we're supposed to be.

In the Marvel Comics Universe, Thor is known, at least to himself, as The Strongest Avenger. This is how he sees himself. He's unbeatable, a true warrior, one who never loses in battle. And then Thanos comes and rocks his whole existence. Thor, for the first time, loses. When he first faces Thanos, he gets beat down on his own ship. He watches as Thanos kills his brother and his friends with his bare hands while he can do nothing. Thanos then escapes and tears Earth to shreds. When Thor finally gets his opportunity to kill Thanos, he misses the mark! He throws his giant battle axe and hits Thanos right in the chest, thinking he'd won. However, Thanos responds with, "You should have gone for the head," as he snaps his fingers and disintegrates half of the population across the universe. Thor lost big time. To himself, not only did he fail, he became a failure.

The movie then fast forwards five years in the future. As it pans to Thor, we can see that his failure has gotten to him. He's wearing no shirt and fingerless gloves while he plays video games in his run down living room with his friends looking like "melted ice cream." He won't see anyone from his kingdom even though he's "King." When the Hulk shows up to ask for his help, he denies his services. He can't even talk about Thanos without being driven to tears. Fortunately, because there is beer and cheese wiz on Hulk's ship, Thor accepts the invitation to fight and joins them on their quest.

As part of their plan to go back in time to reverse what Thanos had done to the universes, Thor has to go back to Asgard to get one of the infinity stones. When he's there, he runs into his mother, who, on that day in the past, is killed. Although Thor tries to hide from his mother, she finds him and immediately recognizes that "the future has not been kind to [him]." She, like any good mother, sits him down, talks to him, and pulls the truth out of his soul:

> *Thor: I was just standing there. Some idiot with an axe.*

> *Frigga: Now, you're no idiot. You're here, aren't you? Seeking counsel from the wisest person in Asgard.*

> *Thor: I am. Yes.*

> *Frigga: Idiot? No. A failure? Absolutely.*

> *Thor: That's a little bit harsh.*

> *Frigga: Do you know what that makes you? Just like everyone else.*

> *Thor: I'm not supposed to be like everyone else, am I?*

Thor has an image of himself that he can't let go of. He's not supposed to be like everyone else. He's supposed to be bigger, stronger, faster, better. He's the king of Asgard. He's the mightiest hero in the universe. At least that's who he thinks he's supposed to be for everyone else. But then his mother hits him with the truth that finally sets him free.

# FRIGGA: EVERYONE FAILS AT WHO THEY ARE SUPPOSED TO BE, THOR. THE MEASURE OF A PERSON, OF A HERO... IS HOW WELL THEY SUCCEED AT BEING WHO THEY ARE.

This, to me, is the most beautiful scene in the entire Marvel Comics Universe. It may actually be a top five scene of all time for me. That's because this is so real and relatable that you can't escape it. I don't know one person alive or who ever lived that has not felt this way at some point. That has not felt the pressure of living up to someone they didn't want to be because the world around them forced them to become someone they're not. Everyone, at some point in their lives, feels this, and that's why this conversation is so beautiful - because it's real. And Frigga gives us all the release that we need to be who we are when she says, "The measure of a person, of a hero... is how well they succeed at being who they are."

With this guidance from his wise mother, Thor goes back to fight and defeat Thanos with the rest of the Avengers. At the end of the movie, he goes back to his kingdom and does not rule, but gives up the crown. With the guidance of his mother reverberating in his head, he admits that he never really wanted to be king. Instead, he runs off with the band of misfits that are the Guardians of the Galaxy. Thor can finally be himself and be happy with that.

As corny as this sounds, this really stuck with me. It got me thinking, "Man, Thor was being someone he didn't want to be for hundreds, if not thousands of years! I don't have that much time to figure out who I want to be. I better start living the way I want now." Again, I know it's corny, but there is great truth in this thought. We don't have a lot of time. We never know which day is going to be our last.

# IF WE WANT TO CAPITALIZE ON OUR LIFE HERE AND THE HAPPINESS WE'RE SUPPOSED TO EXPERIENCE, WE BETTER START FAILING AT WHO WE'RE SUPPOSED TO BE AND SUCCEEDING AT LIVING AS WE REALLY ARE.

Failing at who we're supposed to be drives us to the center of the Mastery Cycle. Remember, YOU are at the center of that cycle. But in order to control that cycle - your thoughts, your words, your actions, etc., you have to be the one in charge. If you are at the mercy of the world around you constantly telling you who to be, you are not the one in charge of your Mastery Cycle. Others control your thoughts, your words are simply repeats of others, your actions are driven by others to satisfy others. Not only is that not who you really are, that's a prison. To set yourself free, you have to fail.

Failing at who you are supposed to be allows you to become who you are meant to be.

# THIS TYPE OF FAILURE IS ADDITION VIA SUBTRACTION - ADDING TO YOUR LIFE THROUGH THE SUBTRACTION OF UNNEEDED CRAP.

That crap is the expectation and desires of others on how you should live your life. Your life is yours and should be viewed as such, for that is where true freedom is found.

Now before we get further into the weeds here, I'm not telling you to give everyone the finger and wander off into doing whatever you want in every moment. That's not freedom, either. That's recklessness. What I'm saying is that by telling other people "no", you free yourself to tell yourself "yes." What we often fail to realize is that for every "yes" we give, we unknowingly say "no" to a countless number of other options. If someone invites you to a party and you say yes, you've booked yourself for that evening. If anything else comes up, you are forced to say no. People knowing that you said yes to one thing may not even ask you to take part in another. Now you've missed that opportunity.

## FOR EVERY "YES" WE GIVE, THERE IS AT LEAST ONE "NO" WE GIVE SIMULTANEOUSLY.

The same holds true for ourselves. If your parents want you to be a doctor, and you say yes, you've said no to every other option. If your friends want you to be a soccer player, you've given up other sports. If the world wants you to be an anxious, hyperemotional mess that is constantly reacting to the media and opinions of others forcing you to make emotional decisions on their behalf, I can guarantee you that you are saying "no" to being in control of yourself, and doing so emphatically.

# THIS TYPE OF LIFESTYLE, ONE LIVED FOR AND DETERMINED BY OTHERS, IS WHAT I CALL BEING AN INDIVIDU-ALL. AT THE CENTER OF YOUR MASTERY CYCLE EXISTS A BEING THAT IS BUSY TRYING TO FULFILL EVERYONE ELSE'S DREAMS, DESIRES, VISIONS, NEEDS, AND PASSIONS, ALL WHILE BEING VOID OF YOUR OWN. WHEN YOU SAY "YES" TO THE INDIVIDU-ALL, YOU SAY "NO" TO YOU AS YOUR OWN INDIVIDUAL.

For the sake of personal recognition, let's define the individu-du-ALL and the individual. Try to identify which one you are right now. Before we can fix something, we must recognize that it's broken…

An Individu-ALL is one who cares deeply about what those around them think about them. One who puts the input of the group above the input that their gut or heart may tell them. One who conforms to peer pressure when they know what they're doing is wrong. One who betrays themselves in order to fit in. In short, an Individu-ALL is not one, but one comprising many that contradicts one's true nature. An Individual, on the other hand, is "a single human being as distinct from a group, class, or family." One who is distinct – "recognizably different in nature from something else of a similar type."

# THE INDIVIDUAL IS YOU, NOT WHO YOU'RE SUPPOSED TO BE BASED ON THE VIEW OR EXPECTATIONS OF OTHERS. AT THIS POINT IN YOUR LIFE, WHICH ONE ARE YOU?

As Brené Brown shared, "the opposite of belonging is fitting in." When we are trying to fit in, we are forced to be what the group expects us to be, often leading to that betrayal of self. But when we belong, we are expected to be our authentic self - our own individual.

This begs the question - how do you find out who you are as an individual? That's a significant question, and one we've already begun to answer.

Let's go back to the previous exercises.

- Chapter 1 exercise was to create your own mantra. What can you repeat to yourself to bring you back to your center? What can you think to yourself when things get hard or uncertain that brings you back to a place of confidence and hope? Define that mantra.

- Chapter 2 exercise was to Name to Tame and Aim your inner voices. As you name the negativity in your mind, you tame it and control it. As you name the positivity in your mind, you aim to direct your actions. What names did you assign to those voices? Who are you aiming at becoming? Which actions do you need to take to get you there?

- Chapter 3 exercise was to write 100 questions to find out what's important to you. What things come to your mind and heart that matter to you? No one has to see this, so you should seek to be as authentic with yourself as possible. After all, this is to help YOU find YOU within these questions.

With these three exercises, you are well on your way to discover who you are as an individual. To add on to that, I want to ask you the following questions: If no one else's opinion of you mattered, what would you do with your life? If there was no possibility of failure, what would you do? What is so important to you that failing at it is better than not attempting at all? Answering these questions will help point you in the right direction towards who you are at the center of your Mastery Cycle.

You may not know the answers to those questions right away. That's okay! That simply means that you need to spend time in the discovery phase, and that can be one of the greatest phases of your life. You get to try new things, experience new passions, and weed out what doesn't work. With time, you will find answers to these questions as you seek them.

Here's the thing though - life doesn't exist in a vacuum. So while you may answer that question confidently while you're on your own, to live it out in real life is entirely different. For example, if I could do anything or be anyone, I would be a cowboy out on my thousand acre ranch with the ability to disappear from the world as I pleased. I would use this ranch to expand the work within this book. I would provide classes around overcoming and optimizing while providing an escape from the world. I would continue to write, provide classes, and teach people how to constantly become stronger than their pain, all to develop personal strength to eventually strengthen others. I would live out my calling of helping others learn to master themselves in order to master their lives.

But, at least as of writing this book, that's not possible with the life choices I've made. I have a wonderful wife who loves sunny California and having a lot of social interaction. I have three beautiful daughters who need an excellent education and a powerful community to give them opportunities in their future. I have to provide for them with my current 9-5 job.

# I HAVE TO DO WHAT IS NECESSARY BEFORE I CAN DO WHAT IS DESIRED.

My answer of "lonesome cowboy" cannot be fully lived within my current reality. However, while I can't do all the things I want to do yet, I can still be the person I want to be within reason, and drive towards my ultimate goal of living out my calling in every moment.

When I talk about becoming the truest individual you can be, I'm not talking about outward expression. Sure, that's part of it. We all need to express outwardly who we are within. But that is surface level. I'm talking about going deeeeeeeeeep within to discover who you are at your core. When I talk about what you want to do with your life, we must remove color, race, sexual orientation, or financial status. Those don't define YOU. Your calling, your purpose, doesn't care about any of those things. In order to discover who we really are, what we are meant to do, and who we are meant to become, we need to remove this outer shell we think defines us and discover who we are without it. Only then can we truly become our own individual.

Now, if you don't know how to answer those questions just yet, you can focus on the process of elimination, furthering addition through subtraction, by answering the following: If you don't know what you want to do just yet, at least tell me what you don't want to do.

Rather than trying to do a bunch of new things to become this whole new person you want to be, or at least think you want to be, let's start some place simpler. Stop doing the things you know you don't like. Start FAILING at what you hate doing. Start FAILING at achieving everyone else's expectations of you. Fail at who you're supposed to be. You can't make everyone happy. It's simply impossible, so stop trying.

One way that we can begin to fail at who we're supposed to be so that we can become who we're meant to be is to, once again, focus on what we can control - that being our perception of self. As Thomas Cooley put it when it comes to how we see ourselves:

# "I AM NOT WHO YOU THINK I AM. I AM NOT WHO I THINK I AM. I AM WHO I THINK YOU THINK I AM."

Often, we see ourselves through the perception of how we believe others see us. That's a lot to unpack. We see ourselves through the eyes of others based on how we think they perceive us. What in that statement shows any semblance of control of self? That's like staring at the center of your Mastery Cycle through a mirror that reflects the mirror reflecting the source. We can't control others' thoughts, emotions, words, or actions, yet we think about ourselves as how we think others view us. To top that off, do we ever ask what we think the other person is thinking about how we're perceived by them? STOP! Stop putting thoughts of who you are into others people's heads about how you think they think about you. That is something we should aim to fail at right now.

The truth is, most people that we think are thinking about us aren't. They simply don't think about us, at least not nearly as much as we think they do. Ask yourself this - taking a subjective spectator perspective, how often do you fixate about others to where you wish you could change them in every waking moment of your day? I'm guessing that the answer is "hardly ever" because you're too worried about yourself. We all are. But when we project our thoughts about what others think about us onto others, we give our integrity of self away. For this reason, we should start here.

# STOP FOCUSING ON WHAT YOU THINK OTHERS THINK OF YOU, AND START FOCUSING ON WHAT YOU THINK OF YOU, FOR THAT IS ALL THAT REALLY MATTERS. IT'S ALSO THE ONLY THING WE CAN CONTROL.

Of course, this all takes practice. A lot of it. And with that, comes time. A lot of it. The process of self-discovery is just that - a process. It's not something that is going to happen overnight. And within the process, you're going to fail at failing at who you're supposed to be. That's okay. Keep going. Try again. Stopping never got anybody closer to their goal, and it won't get you closer to yours. As the saying goes, "practice makes perfect," and while we'll never truly attain perfection, "practice makes improvement" will always hold true.

We are always a work in progress, but the progress that we desire to make within ourselves comes from the action of constantly working on ourselves. Sure, we need to take time to think about what's important to us, who we want to become, and how we want to get there, but then we need to live it.

# YOU NEED TO GIVE YOURSELF THE PERMISSION TO STOP BEING WHAT EVERYONE WANTS YOU TO BE IN ORDER TO GIVE YOURSELF TIME AND SPACE TO DISCOVER WHO YOU WANT TO BE.

A pottery teacher illustrated the power of this point - the difference in practice vs. theory - with one of his classes[9]. At the beginning

of the semester, he divided his Intro to Pottery class i
Group 1 was asked to make as much pottery as they co
to get an "A" was 50 pounds of pottery made. To get a
have to make 40 pounds. To get a "C", 30 pounds, a
2 was asked to make the perfect pot. They only had t
but it had to be perfect. At the end of the semester, w
made the best looking pot? Group 1! Specifically, t
50 pounds of pottery! Why? Because through thei
practice, they got better. Group 2 watched videos on
perfect pot, drew sketches of what they wanted it to
at other pots made my other people to find what the p
contain, but they never got their hands dirty until it ca
the "perfect pot."

## WITHOUT THE PRACTICE AND THE UNAVOIDA THAT COMES AT THE BEGINNING OF TRYING SO GROUP 2 HADN'T LEARNED ENOUGH ABOUT TH TRULY MAKE A PERFECT POT.

While this story is great to illustrate the powe
theory, sometimes life deals you a hand that shatte
made. Perhaps, as was my experience with the pas
mother, life shatters the 30 pounds of pots you we
targeted your 50 pounds for an "A". Unfortunately
this happens to the best of us. When this happens,
response is to throw it all away and stop making mo
what I'm asking you to do, telling you to do, is to
and rebuild.

Kintsugi is a Japanese philosophy and practice that addresses life experience head on. When life shatters your pottery, rather than throwing it all away, take the shards that remain and put them back together with gold. That's actually what Kintsugi means - "golden repair." When you take this approach, your once broken vase becomes more valuable.

## WHAT WOULD BE SEEN AS CRACKS AND UGLY SCARS ARE NOW VIEWED AS BEAUTY AND INCREASED VALUE AS THE GOLD SHINES IN THEIR PLACE.

This is how failing at who you're supposed to be can feel - like you're shattering all the pots you've spent so much time making. And before you can continue to build the new pots, you must first repair the ones that you have shattered. This takes time, patience, fortitude, resilience, confidence, and every other good virtue in the book. But as you rebuild with the mindset of Kintsugi, you will ultimately make yourself more valuable and more beautiful than before.

We are constantly a wet ball of clay that is waiting to be molded. The type of pot we become is determined by who is doing the shaping. If you have 10 people trying to shape one pot, it's going to fall apart because each person is going to change what it's supposed to look like.

But if you take charge, grab the wheel, and begin to mold yourself, you will be the one dictating who you become. In the process, you're going to mess up. That's fine. Just keep shaping. Eventually, through constantly trying to make a "perfect pot", you'll make a version of you that you are proud of. But to start becoming who you want to be, you first have to fail at who you're supposed to be.

# CHAPTER ACTIVITY
## A LETTER FROM FUTURE YOU

When I was 15 and a freshman in high school, I was given the assignment to write myself a letter from my future self, specifically the future senior class-man version of me, to the freshman me. Here is what that letter said:

*Dear me,*

*How are you?... I'm betting the next time I read this I'll be 6'2",*
*between 175 and 200 pounds. I want to have gone out with Ashley*
*Amos because she is the hottest girl I know. When you read this, thank*
*your family and friends for everything. Thank Jeremiah for being*
*your inspiration and for all that he did for you... Go get a tattoo and*
*call Ashley Amos.... Make sure you always remember the good times.*
*Always have fun and always live life to the fullest...."*

Let's bullet the tasks that my senior self told my freshman self to accomplish:

- Grow to 175-200 pounds
- Thank family, specifically Jeremiah
- Get tattoos
- Remember the good times (be grateful)
- Live life to the fullest
- Call Ashley Amos and go out with her

Today, while it's many years after my senior year of high school, I am 195 pounds and covered in tattoos. CHECK. I constantly thank Jeremiah and the rest of my family for being there for me, and boy, have they been there for me. CHECK. Remember the good times, be grateful, and live life to the fullest - all of that is wrapped up in this book and my everyday life through gratitude practices and raising my children. CHECK. Finally, call and go out with Ashley Amos. She's now my wife, and still an absolute smoke show. FRICKIN CHECK!

Unbeknownst to me, I had tapped into a secret I was unaware of - I had connected the future me with the current me on a deeper level. With this exercise, I had expressed to myself who I wanted to be - grateful, powerful, strong, supported - and who I wanted to be those things with - Ashley. Still can't believe I bagged me such a woman. Anyway, with this exercise, I had a clearer path laid before me on who I wanted to become.

The exercise for this chapter is for you to do the same. I want you to write a letter to current self from your future self. As we acknowledged, the future version of us should be a far better version of us than who we are currently. You + two years of life experience should be better than you now. If you're so inclined, have this letter be from the best version of you and use the name you've given that best version from the previous chapter's exercise.

The purpose of this exercise is to start the outline for who you want to be so that you can begin to fail at who you're supposed to be. In this letter, be as clear as you can. Write your hopes and dreams, how you intend to get there, who's there with you, what type of attitude you have, what trials or challenges have you overcome in the time between, who you have failed to be in order to become who you are meant to be, and the virtues you now embody as the "best" version of you. Write it all down, get it out on paper, and don't be afraid to turn it in to your closest friends and family like I had to turn it in to my teacher. Share it with those that you believe will help you achieve the goals that you are setting and connecting to. You'll need them on your journey - what a perfect time to invite them to join you in becoming the best version of yourself.

Take it a step further than I did with mine at 15 and review this letter you have written yourself every 3-6 months. Give yourself the opportunity to adjust your actions to meet your goals. In fact, give yourself the opportunity to adjust your goals if needed. Make them more accurate and defined, make them bigger, and if required, read-just your target. Reviewing this letter every so often will allow you to remind yourself who you are trying to become and will be a shield to you against the person you're "supposed" to be.

You have the potential to be great, the absolute best you can be, if you work towards that.

BUT TO DO THAT, YOU HAVE TO SAY "NO" TO WHO YOU'RE SUPPOSED TO BE AS DEFINED BY OTHERS, AND DEFINE THE PATH YOU NEED TO WALK TO BECOME WHO YOU'RE MEANT TO BE. IT'S IN YOUR POWER, WHICH MEANS IT'S YOUR RESPONSIBILITY. WHO ARE YOU MEANT TO BE?

# CHAPTER 5
## INNER MOUNTAINS OF MASTERY | PHYSICAL

"NO CITIZEN HAS A RIGHT TO BE AN AMATEUR IN THE MATTER OF PHYSICAL TRAINING... WHAT A DISGRACE IT IS FOR A MAN [OR WOMAN] TO GROW OLD WITHOUT EVER SEEING THE BEAUTY AND STRENGTH OF WHICH HIS [OR HER] BODY IS CAPABLE."
- SOCRATES

For the last 12 years, fitness has been my muse, my escape, and my medicine. From Body Building, to CrossFit, to GoRuck, I have pushed myself to find new limits. While in my youth it brought me ferocity, in my adulthood, it brings me peace.

I've mentioned that I'm not the healthiest on the inside. However, with my washboard abs that I've never had to work that hard for, you could never tell. Between my asthma, my eosinophilic esophagitis (EE), and my crohn's, I'm not what you would call a "high performance athlete." But I have always wanted to be, so I continue to push myself to find MY limits.

In 2022, I expanded what I deemed personally possible and decided to try to run a marathon. Running has never been my forte, and for good reasons. One - I'm a daily asthmatic who's best friends with his inhaler. Two - my Crohn's historically freaks out on me after about five miles (I'm being polite when saying that). And three - running is dumb. But, to push myself, I thought, "hey, since you've never run more than 5 miles at one time in your life, why don't you run a marathon? That should be an enjoyable learning experience!" I couldn't have been more right and more wrong at the same time.

For months I trained for this marathon. I watched all the videos I could on proper form, diet, breathing, and equipment - whatever I could get my hands on, I would study. I would watch hours of David Goggins and listen to his book "Can't Hurt Me" over and over while I ran. Ten miles became easy and my body was adjusting. I was feeling good. So far in my training, my asthma was fine and my Crohn's seemed to adjust. Aside from a bit of discomfort around 15 miles, I seemed to do okay. Then came my first "long run." Eighteen miles was the target.

Eighteen miles hit differently than anything I had previously run. At the end, my body freaked out. Physically I seemed fine - muscles didn't hurt, breathing was good, heart rate was on target. But then I stopped and waited for my wife to pick me up with our daughters so we could head to the beach. Things began to go dark.

When I have my Crohn's flair ups, I get nauseous and start throwing up everything in my stomach. I get a fever and cold chills regardless of the outside temperature. I get sweaty and my body convulses as I sit there and wait for it all to pass. There's not much that I can do. After 18 miles, I felt this coming on.

Luckily, some cold water and ice on my core, and some breathing exercises slowed everything down enough to prevent a flair up. Sure, the walls caved in around me. I started seeing black. I got full chills while I sweated through my shorts in an air-conditioned car, and I was breathing back dry heaves. But comparatively speaking, I was good. We went to the beach and had a great day. This should have been a warning sign. I, in my infinite wisdom, ignored it.

The day of the marathon had arrived. My buddy and I jumped on the first bus at 04:00 and headed to the start line. The race didn't start until 07:00, but we wanted to be there and mentally primed for our big run.

While we waited in the freezing Utah mountains for our race to start, I ran through my plan in my head. "Keep feet lubed, stay hydrated, and stay fueled. Don't worry about everyone else's pace. Stick to your plan and run your own race. Don't let the heat of the moment get to you and come out too hot. Stay in control. Aim for 9-10 minute miles for the first 13 miles, then bust it on the last half since it's mostly downhill. No music until you need it, and that shouldn't be until half way. Remember your why and stay focused. You got this." I felt like I did have it.

At 0700 the sound of the gun rang through the air. We all started moving slowly like a herd of cows, but eventually everything opened up. I was passed left and right by small children and old ladies. "Don't worry, Alex. Run your race. You have 26 miles to go." I was in control.

Miles stacked up, and before I knew it, I was approaching the first big hill before the halfway mark. My plan was not to walk it, but to slowly trod, and I would pass all those people that passed me at the start. My thought was that those suckers would be burned out by here, and I was right. I slowly proceeded up the hill at my pace and passed many people that had previously passed me. Losers. My plan was being executed flawlessly. High five to me.

Before I knew it, I was approaching the top of the hill, right around 13 miles - the halfway point. I was right on schedule for me, and that had included a pee break in some well hydrated bushes. I was on fire and feeling good, mainly because I knew some downhill was coming. I had studied the maps and watched YouTube videos on the course. I knew what was in front of me and was looking forward to it.

I turned my music on and began cranking down some hills. I was on pace, making up time, and sticking to my plan. I had water at every station, and Gatorade at every other. I was having gummies where I could get them and was avoiding any type of cramping. My plan was working! And then it wasn't. Like Mike Tyson says, "Everyone has a plan until they get punched in the mouth," and that's just what happened. Who's the loser now?

My wife and friends were waiting for me at mile 16. I couldn't wait to see them - I needed the moral support of my wife and newborn daughter. I was behind schedule, but I was determined to keep going. They later told me that at that mile marker, they could see that I was struggling, but they hoped their support would keep me going. It did.

At mile 18, just like in training, I realized that something was building up inside me I wouldn't be able to reverse if I didn't stop. Again, being the wise, physical specimen that I am, I continued to push, remembering Lao Tsū's quote, "It doesn't matter how slowly you go, as long as you do not stop." I was not going to stop.

But then mile 20 hit, and I realized I was going into a flair up. All the bouncing from running down hill hit harder than I expected. My plan of accelerating downhill had backfired. The walls began to close in, my mouth started to salivate to prepare for the vomit, which I couldn't do since I had nothing left in my system. The chills started as I sweated in 75 degree weather. Still, I was determined to keep going. They were going to have to peel me off the pavement before I took the bus of shame back to the start line.

As I approached mile 23 slowly and zombie like, an angel with the job of a nurse called out to me by name. "Hey, Alex. How you doin', bud?" Being so focused on not passing out, I kept my eyes on my feet and mind on my breathing and replied slowly, "Not good." She raced over to me and helped me over to the side. As soon as I stopped moving, it all hit.

I began to convulse uncontrollably, per usual. She wrapped me in a blanket, gave me some water, and covered me in ice from head to core, trying to bring down my internal temperature. She had oxygen at this station, which she used on me for the better part of an hour to keep me over oxygenated to feed my struggling body. At this point, I was wondering if this was the end of the line for me.

I began to tear up. As my body shook, the tears fell and the nurses and aids there couldn't help but pity me. They asked me at least 3 times if I wanted to get on a bus back, going as far as stopping one and trying to help me up to get into it, which I adamantly refused. I had come this far. I was not going to quit.

The tears were not due to the thought of not finishing for a medal or bragging rights. I could always come back and run a marathon with a different plan and more slowly. Besides, no one would fault me for stopping now. Having a flair up is out of my control. I had truly given it all that I had. Or so I thought.

This is where I had to dig deep into my WHY. When the rest of my plan had blown up, my why remained. I had put months of training in at the expense of family time, my wife's over abundance of support, and playing with my daughters. I had spent money on new gear, travel, and accommodations. I had suckered my buddy to run this with me. I had friends come watch and support me. I had invested hours of training and study into this. I would not let that go to waste. Most importantly, I was not going to let those down who believed in me.

As I recovered, I continued to breathe and dig deep. I crafted a new plan - wait for my buddy to catch up and we would cross the finish line together. Thank goodness for him, because without him, I probably wouldn't have finished.

About an hour after I got there, my buddy met me at the aid station and helped me get up. From that point on, we would walk as far as needed, then jog as far as I could. I held an icepack on my core to keep me cool until we crossed the finish line just under the 6 hour mark. Feeling broken, I knew I had given it my all. I could go home the next day proudly, knowing I left it all out on the road. Challenge accepted. Challenge completed.

---

I share this story to illustrate the power of physical activities when it comes to mastering ourselves. I call this approach the Inner Mountains of Mastery. These mountains, Physical, Mental, Emotional, Intuitional, and Spiritual, are the next step in the process of becoming stronger than our pain. In addition to the Mastery Cycles, these mountains put us on the path to recognizing and then striving to become our best selves.

It took everything I had across each Inner Mountain of Mastery - Physical, Mental, Emotional, Intuitional and Spiritual - to finish this marathon. In the Five Inner Mountains of Mastery, the Physical Mountain is the one we should start climbing first. Let me share why.

When I speak to the Physical Mountain, I want to start by stating that this is not the Fitness Mountain. Yes, exercise and movement are key, but there are many parts to our physical well-being. Sleeping enough, eating well, and moving constantly being the foundational three. And, in my opinion, that is the order of importance. Why? Well, with one dreadful night of sleep, your performance is diminished, decreasing your movement goal and physical capacity. Miss sleep consistently and you're in a world of hurt. You give into cravings because your will power is lowered, which means you eat poorly, too much, or not enough. Sleep affects the other two.

Having been in the bodybuilding and fitness industry for many years, the saying goes, "You can't out train a poor diet." And that's true. You can workout a ton, but if what you're consuming is not on par with your goals, then you won't attain them. On top of that, it affects your sleep if you're eating poorly, too much, too little, or too late. Eating is number two.

Then, after these two pillars, we come to movement. When I say movement, I don't mean going to the gym for two hours a day. In fact, I don't mean going to the gym at all, if that's not for you. But you have to move every single day and as much as you can. Before I get into the weeds here, let's break each one of these down.

When it comes to our sleep, I cannot emphasize it enough that you have to get at least seven hours a night. If you're an adolescent, you need more with a minimum of 8-9. Often, as life gets stressful, our sleep is the first thing we give up. Me included. We work late into the night, or in my case, I wake up at 04:00 to sneak in a few extra hours of work, providing myself with only 6ish hours of sleep. Over time, this becomes toxic.

Pertaining to our mental performance and our willpower, sleep is paramount. Our brains, like other organs in our bodies, need rest and to be cleansed. We do detoxes to clean our gut and stomach. We'll hit the steam room and sauna to sweat out toxins. We'll fast to give our bodies rest from overconsumption. But regarding our brains, the main thing that cleanses the brain is sleep.

The big thing I want to focus on in this book is that sleep increases your willpower. As we strive to overcome self-doubt, anxiety, and depression, that willpower is absolutely critical.

# WILLPOWER IS YOUR ABILITY TO DO WHAT YOU KNOW IS NECESSARY EVEN IF YOU DON'T WANT TO DO IT. IT'S ALSO YOUR ABILITY TO RESIST SOMETHING DETRIMENTAL. "WHERE THERE'S A WILL, THERE'S A WAY," CAN ALSO BE VIEWED AS, "WHERE THERE'S NO WILL, THERE'S NO WAY."

Without our willpower, or synonymously our grit, self-discipline, self-control, or drive, overcoming the weight we must shoulder to master ourselves becomes too heavy to bear. Without it, we may not be stronger than our pain. Therefore, sleep is crucial, and is the first pillar and foundation that the other pillars of the Physical Mountain stand on, especially in our 24/7/365 world.

The reason this is so important is because of what happens to the brain when we sleep. Our sleep, as previously mentioned, cleanses the brain and helps it recover. The performance of our Prefrontal Cortex is directly related to our sleep performance. More sleep = greater Prefrontal Cortex performance. Cool, but why is this important to master ourselves and overcome self doubt, anxiety, and depression?

Our Prefrontal Cortex (PFC) is directly responsible for nine specific things: bodily regulation, attuned communication, emotional balance, response flexibility, fear modulation, empathy, insight, moral awareness and intuition. All of these things tie into our ability to overcome self-doubt, anxiety, and depression.

# SO AS OUR SLEEP PERFORMANCE DECREASES, SO DOES OUR PFC PERFORMANCE, LEADING TO A DECREASE IN OUR ABILITY TO REGULATE AND CONTROL OUR EMOTIONAL RESPONSES.

Bringing this back to Chapter One, what do we need to control first and foremost if we're to control our Mastery Cycle? Our attitude. And what is our attitude? A combination of our thoughts and emotions. Again, we've come full circle.

To further the need for sleep, our PFC is not the only part of our brain that is affected when sleep suffers. The PFC is directly connected to the Limbic System. Our Limbic System is where our Autonomic Nervous System lives. This controls our fight / flight / freeze response, otherwise known as our Sympathetic or Parasympathetic Response. The Limbic System is responsible for this response center, as well as being a home to our emotions. So if we aren't getting our sleep, our Limbic System that houses our emotions and our stress responses gets out of whack, leading us to have trouble relaxing and settling into a parasympathetic state where anxiety is decreased. Convinced that your sleep is of the utmost importance yet? Let's keep going.

Your willpower is a muscle, and while it's infinite, it needs to be recharged frequently. Studies have proven that our "resources become exhausted when repeated acts of self-control occur, much as a muscle become fatigued following physical exertion." These resources include our mental, emotional, and physical energies. These are our virtues and character traits, such as patience, kindness, empathy, and discipline. When we constantly have to use our willpower, we exhaust it, especially at the start of this journey. We refer to this type of exhaustion of willpower and internal resources as Ego Depletion[10]. Ego, while typically seen in a negative light, is needed to be successful.

# EGO IS DEFINED AS A PERSON'S SENSE OF SELF-ESTEEM OR SELF-IMPORTANCE, AND IF WE'RE TRYING TO OVERCOME SELF DOUBT, WE NEED TO FEED OUR EGO HEALTHY FUEL TO HELP IT GROW TO BATTLE OUR INNER NEGATIVITY. EGO DEPLETION IS UNACCEPTABLE.

To add insult to injury, the Limbic System is attached to our Amygdala. Our Amygdala houses our sensory receptors, primarily those with fear and threats. When we are sleep deprived, our brain's ability to reduce the Amygdala's activity is reduced, leading to an over focus on the negative as a survival response. AKA - we perceive more negativity around us. And as we've learned already, what you PERCEIVE is what you ACHIEVE.

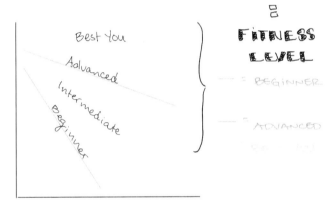

**EGO DEPLETION**

WILL-POWER
SELF-CONTROL,
GRIT,
DISCIPLINE

Best You
Advanced
Intermediate
Beginner

GAP
=
FITNESS LEVEL

BEGINNER

ADVANCED

**EXERTION**
HOW HARD YOU'VE WORKED /
HOW MANY PSYCHOLOGICAL
RESOURCES YOU'VE USED
UP TODAY

While the graph is theoretical in its data, it's accurate in its principle. When we start on this journey to become the master of ourselves, our learning curve is steep, and therefore takes a lot of willpower to start. This leads to quicker depletion of that resource. Over time, we put in practice and our fitness level improves. I'm not talking about physical fitness like bench press. I'm talking about overall fitness of self - our willpower endurance increases. Eventually, our willpower can withstand almost anything as long as its fuel is being maintained. And while we will never live up to the green line, it's something we can always strive to achieve.

Let's put it all together now:

# TO OVERCOME SELF DOUBT, ANXIETY, AND / OR DEPRESSION WE NEED AS MUCH WILLPOWER, OR SELF CONTROL, AS WE CAN MUSTER. THE RESOURCES THAT FUEL OUR WILLPOWER ARE PRIMARILY HOUSED IN OUR PREFRONTAL CORTEX, LIMBIC SYSTEM, AND AMYGDALA. WHEN WE NEGLECT OUR SLEEP, THE PERFORMANCE OF THESE CENTERS IN THE BRAIN FOLLOW SUIT, LEADING TO A DECREASE IN OUR RESOURCES TO FUEL OUR WILLPOWER. THIS DECREASE IN RESOURCES LEADS TO EGO DEPLETION, OR A DEPLETION IN SELF-ESTEEM OR SELF-IMPORTANCE. THIS DECREASE IN SELF-IMPORTANCE FUELS BUSTER AND ALLOWS HIM TO BEAT YOU TO A PULP.

Long story short - GET YOUR SLEEP!

Following our need to sleep is the need to eat well, whatever that means to you. And I mean that - whatever works for you is what is going to work best.

There are endless amounts of diets out there that all claim to be the best - Vegan, Carnivore, Vegetarian, Pescatarian. And there are countless plans that claim to work better than the rest - If It Fits Your Macros (IIFYM), Intermittent Fasting (IF), Keto, Low Carb, so forth and so on. So which Nutritional Discipline is best for you? I call it a Nutritional Discipline rather than a diet, because that is the key to success here. It has to be a discipline that you are consistent with. It can't be a temporary diet you go all in on for a month and then pull out of the next. Discipline and consistency are key.

Recent Meta-Studies have provided answers to this question - "Which is best?11" It's ground breaking and may, in fact, rock your entire world. They have found, drum roll please, that the best diet that you can follow is the one that you can stick with the longest. BOOM! Ground breaking discovery! Yeah… but not really. Thank you, Captain Obvious.

I don't want to downplay the effort that went in to this study - it was a lot. To collect all the data to draw the conclusion of which diet is best, 59 articles were included, 48 randomized controlled trials were done, which included 7,286 participants. The study reviewed 11 different named diets, capturing the main diet approaches of macronutrients, low-carb, and low-fat, along with the control group of "no diet." Again, this was a lot of work, and in the end, the honest answer was the one that we need as individuals:

# "THIS STUDY PROVIDES VERY STRONG CONFIRMATION OF WHAT IS ANECDOTALLY KNOWN AMONG MOST PROFESSIONALS IN THE FIELD: WHATEVER DIET A PERSON CAN STICK WITH IS THE BEST DIET FOR THEM..."

Within the study, they included Frequently Asked Questions, one of which was, "If every diet works, why diet at all? Why not just eat healthy foods?" It's a great question that comes back to our Mastery Cycle and our Physical Mountain of Mastery. It's not just the diet that we choose, but the mentality and the discipline that comes with it. When we don't choose a Nutritional Discipline to follow, we consume without consequences or guidelines, leading us to stray. The mindset that comes with choosing a discipline to stick to traverses the food itself to other aspects of our lives that we should not overlook.

So why is this important to overcome self doubt, anxiety, and depression, and how does it help us become stronger than our pain?

During fetal production, our brain and our gut are grown from the same tissues, which is why we can refer to the gut as the body's second brain. Because of that, the gut produces many of our key hormones, leading to our emotional well-being. Major happiness hormones, such as Serotonin and Dopamine, live in our gut.

# IN FACT, 90% OF OUR SEROTONIN, OR OUR HAPPY HORMONE, LIVES IN THE GUT. 50% OF OUR DOPAMINE, WHICH IS RESPONSIBLE FOR FEELINGS, REWARDS, AND MOTIVATION, LIVES IN THE GUT.

Other hormones that live in the gut are:

- 5-HT: "In the Central Nervous System, it can also act as a neurotransmitter to regulate mood, sleep, and appetite."

- NPY: "...affects stress-related disorders, neuroprotection, neuroinflammation, and neurogenesis.... and participate in the modulation of anxiety and depression."

- GLP-1: "...best known as a hormone stimulating glucose-dependent insulin secretion, also responds to stress."

- CCK: "It seems that CCK modulates mood disorders through other neurotransmitters, including glutamate, dopamine, acetylcholine, and GABA, all of which play key roles in emotional behaviors."

- Ghrelin: our hunger hormone "was also identified as a regulator of stress response, anxiety, and depression."

These have all been identified with known roles in mood disorders, such as anxiety and depression.

# LONG STORY SHORT, YOUR SELF DOUBT, ANXIETY, AND DEPRESSION HAVE DIRECT TIES TO WHAT YOU ARE PUTTING INTO YOUR BODY.

As we've been addressing, and will continue to address through this book, you are an individual, not an individu-ALL. That means that you have idiosyncrasies that work for you and may not work for others. That's okay. But with that comes the responsibility to figure out what works best for you. As a rule of thumb, however, I would suggest the following:

- Minimize as much sugar as possible. Not just refined sugar, but all types of sugar. Be aware of pseudo names to disguise sugar, such as corn syrup, nectars, and fructose. If you can cut out processed sugars completely, go for it.

- Cut out gluten and / or processed flours.

- Cut out seed oils completely. This includes, but is not limited to, grapeseed oil, sunflower oil, canola oil, just to name a few.

- Watch your dairy intake, and only consume the best dairy you can get your hands on. Diary is becoming highly processed like wheat and gluten, leading to further intolerances within the body.

- Minimize, if not completely remove, alcohol. If you're dealing with self doubt, anxiety, or depression in any form, avoid alcohol all together. Not only does it mess with your hormones, but it's a depressant and should be avoided at all costs.

Starting with these five points is great, because it focuses on the approach of "addition of self through the subtraction of the unnecessary." When you remove these things, what's left? Whole foods. These things we should avoid are in processed foods. You will be hard pressed to find whole foods with artificial sugars, gluten, or seed oils. From here, you can start playing with a nutritional discipline that works best for you.

We haven't touched on this yet, but it's worth mentioning now:

# IF WE ARE TO BECOME MASTERS OF OURSELVES, ONE OF THE EASIEST WAY TO START THAT PROCESS IS TO BECOME A MASTER OF WHAT WE CONSUME.

If we cannot control our impulses of what we eat and drink, how are we supposed to control other impulses of consumption? What we consume today is not just what we put into our mouths, but what we put into our mind and our spirits. Take social media, for example. It is pure, unadulterated mental and emotional consumption. If we master the discipline of controlling our impulses of what we put into our mouths, we come to gain control over what we put into our minds and spirits.

---

Now for movement. Again, when I say movement, I'm not talking about working out at the gym for two hours a day. In fact, if that is all you do and then you sit on your butt for the rest of the day, that's still not enough. Movement consists of anything that gets us, well, moving. The key is to do it every day, and as many times within that day as you can.

Connecting with movement and exercise, whether that is walking, yoga, swimming, resistance training, etc., it does more than just a body good, it does the mind good. Studies now show that exercise is just as effective as many popular antidepressants, including the ones that I took for years, and have since stopped taking with the use of these tools shared in this book.* (If you are on medications, please consult with your doctor about coming off. This is not medical advice suggesting that you can stop your medications.)

While many studies and meta-studies have been done coming to the same conclusion, I'll share one to highlight the point. This study is the most recent study released (March 2nd, 2023) on the effectiveness of physical activity as it relates to overcoming depression and anxiety.

This study, done in correspondence with the University of South Australia[12], set out to "synthesize the evidence on the effects of physical activity on symptoms of depression, anxiety, and psychological distress in adult populations." Why? Because depression and anxiety are the world's leading causes of mental-health related burdens and disorders, and we need to find a better way to address these issues, as they are forecasted to continue to rise. The annual cost of mental disorders has been estimated to be around $2.5 trillion and is estimated to increase to $6 trillion by 2030. I don't know about you, but I refuse to be a part of this statistic.

This is the first study of its kind to organize such a large body of evidence on the effects of Physical Activity (PA) as it targets depression, anxiety, and psychological stress. It includes 97 reviews, findings of 1,039 RCTs (Randomized Control Trials), all involving 128,119 participants across many demographics and clinical populations. However, regardless of the population, "all PA modes were effective, and higher intensity exercise was associated with greater improvements for depression and anxiety... resistance exercise had the largest effects on depression, while Yoga and other mind-body exercises were most effective for reducing anxiety."

These findings are critical in connection with taking control of our individual situations. So critical, in fact, that the:

# "UNIVERSITY OF SOUTH AUSTRALIA RESEARCHERS ARE CALLING FOR EXERCISE TO BE A MAINSTAY APPROACH FOR MANAGING DEPRESSION AS A NEW STUDY SHOWS THAT PHYSICAL ACTIVITY IS 1.5 TIMES MORE EFFECTIVE THAN COUNSELING OR THE LEADING MEDICATIONS."

Read that again - "1.5 times more effective than counseling or leading medications." Tying back to our Mastery Cycles and controlling our controllables, this is exactly what I'm talking about and WHY. This is absolutely within our control! And the best part - it's more effective than relying on someone or something else to change our situation for us.

I am not recommending that you stop your meds or your current system - that is something you need to discuss with your doctor(s) and your support network. But what I am recommending, and in fact demanding to the extent that I can, is that whatever decision you make, you must decide to add exercise to your daily regimen. This exercise doesn't have to be long. In fact, this study shares that short bursts of intense exercise (High Intensity Interval Training or HIIT) are better to relieve the symptoms of depression than longer training. This can be 15 minutes of intense exercise! And remember, intense is by YOUR definition, not by anyone else's. You set your own bar, but then you must set out to raise that bar daily.

Here's the big takeway when climbing the Physical Mountain as your first mountain - it's the bridge to all the other mountains. What you do physically plays directly into the other parts of your being.

# SCIENCE IS NOW BEGINNING TO CONNECT THAT THERE IS NO DIFFERENCE IN PHYSICAL, MENTAL, OR EMOTIONAL HEALTH. WE NEED TO REFRAME THAT AND LOOK AT IT HOLISTICALLY - IT'S JUST HEALTH. IT'S ALL WRAPPED INTO ONE.

When we sleep and eat well, we provide our bodies with the foundation that it needs to balance ourselves chemically to push ourselves physically. As we push ourselves physically, we come to encounter the other parts of our being and use the tools that we develop in real time. Life is full of pain, whether you choose to experience it or not.

# THE PHYSICAL MOUNTAIN ACTS AS A PRACTICE ARENA FOR US TO BRING PAIN UPON OURSELVES AND PRACTICE THE TOOLS THAT WE ARE DEVELOPING. THAT WAY, WHEN LIFE PROVIDES THE PAIN, WE'RE READY TO ENCOUNTER IT HEAD ON AND AVOID SUFFERING.

# IN MY MARATHON, I PUSHED MYSELF BEYOND WHAT I THOUGHT MY BODY WAS CAPABLE OF, GIVEN MY HEALTH CONDITIONS. WHILE I LEARNED I COULD OVERCOME THAT KIND OF PAIN, WHAT I LEARNED ABOUT MYSELF ON A MENTAL, EMOTIONAL, AND SPIRITUAL LEVEL, PARTICULARLY MY WHY, WAS EVEN MORE POWERFUL.

As I sat and asked myself if I could continue, my inner dialogue put the best version of me to the test. It forced me to converse with him in real time while fighting off Buster, who was constantly telling me to quit. I had to practice my breathing and meditation, taking control of the space between stimulus and response. I had to become a subjective spectator to make a good call - the right call about my health vs my desire to finish - relying on my intuition. I had to further that subjective spectator position and consider the time, energy, and love that those who supported me had given and what my failing to complete this task would mean to them. What example did I want to set for my children? How would I see myself in the future if I quit? I faced all of this through this physical challenge, forcing me to BE the person I had desired to BECOME. It brought the future and optimal me into the present, and that is what we need to strive to do in all things.

Let's bring this back to the Mastery Cycle. If you look at the three main things that we can control - our thoughts, our words, and our actions - all three are tied to the confidence that we build as we act according to our desired future self. Our actions dictate our being, which dictates our thoughts and our inner dialog, which further dictates our actions. That continues to revolve around the cycle until we meet our destiny. The fastest way to grab hold of the Mastery Cycle is to act according to our desired being. That desired being must be physically capable if he or she is to take on the demands of the world. They must be healthy in body if they are to be healthy in mind and spirit. Therefore, we must climb the Physical Mountain first.

Finally, the Physical Mountain is the easiest mountain to track and measure. How many hours of sleep are you getting? What did you eat today? How long and how hard did you exercise today? We can measure and compare all of that to our holistic health. And when things are measured and tracked, your performance increases. When looking at those who aimed to walk 10,000 steps per day, studies compared those that tracked versus those that didn't.

## WHAT THEY FOUND WAS THAT THOSE THAT TRACKED THEIR WALKING WALKED AN AVERAGE OF ONE MILE MORE PER DAY THAN THOSE THAT DIDN'T, SIMPLY BECAUSE THEIR TRACKING SHIFTED THEIR MINDSET TO ACHIEVE MORE. MEASURING YOUR PHYSICAL PROGRESS FURTHERS YOUR MENTAL PROGRESS.

If I asked you, "how is your spiritual fitness?" or "what is your mental and emotional endurance like?" what metrics could you give me to illustrate your fitness level on these mountains? They are much harder to articulate and measure, and even if you could measure them, the metric would be physical in nature. "My spiritual level of fitness is great because I meditate every day for 30 minutes." Great - that is a physical act. Almost everything ties back to some form of physical act because we are currently physical beings. Our overall health, wellness, and fitness are all intertwined, starting with the physical.

You don't need to run a marathon or come close to passing out to learn these lessons about yourself. But you do need to push yourself towards personal excellence every day. And remember, that targeted excellence is based on YOUR capabilities at any given time. If I learned anything from my marathon, it's that I will not try to compete with David Goggins in the running arena. That's not for me. You, too, need to find what works for you, and strive to be the best that YOU can be. You need to strive for discipline in what you consume physically, so you can control what you consume mentally, emotionally, and spiritually. And with you pushing as hard as YOU can every day, you need to match that exertion with an equal amount of rest.

# TO CONTROL YOUR MASTERY CYCLE AND THE INDIVIDUAL THAT LIES AT ITS CENTER ACROSS ALL INNER MOUNTAINS OF MASTERY - MENTAL, EMOTIONAL, INTUITIONAL, AND SPIRITUAL - YOU MUST BEGIN THE CLIMB ON THE PHYSICAL.

# CHAPTER ACTIVITY
## DESIGN YOUR PHYSICAL MOUNTAIN

As this chapter illustrates, your Inner Mountains of Mastery are specific to you as an individual. While we can paint in broad strokes what "typically" works for groups, what works best for you is only for you to decide. But with that idiosyncratic approach comes the individual responsibility to do the work you think is best for you. That is what this chapter activity is all about.

If you fail to plan, you better plan to fail. Let's continue to focus on what we can control to get us closer to our desired destiny and take some time to plan out what works best for us.

Let's start with sleep. There's not a lot of room to negotiate. You need at least seven hours of sleep. Not just time in bed, but actual sleep. But what you can negotiate is your wake up time, and then work backward toward your bed and sleep time. For example, I target to wake up at 04:00. That means that I need to be in bed for about eight hours, since I lose anywhere from 30 minutes to 60 minutes of sleep per night having young kids. That then means that I need to be in bed by 20:00 to ensure I get seven hours of sleep at a minimum. You need to do this exercise, too. What time do you want / need to wake up? What time do you need to be in bed? In addition to that, what do you need to do to get ready for bed to help you sleep better? What is your nightly routine like?

Regardless of what you need to do to get ready for bed, what you DON'T need to do is to be on your phone. Focusing on the addition of self through the subtraction of the unnecessary - your phone is unnecessary at night.

# IN FACT, STUDIES ARE CONCRETE IN THEIR FINDINGS THAT BLUE LIGHT AFTER SUNSET THROWS OFF OUR CIRCADIAN RHYTHM AND DISRUPTS OUR SLEEP MORE THAN ANYTHING ELSE.

So regardless of all the other things you need to do, what you need to do the most is put your phone away and remove blue light at least one hour before your targeted bed time. If you can wear blue light blocking glasses during that time, even better.

Now for food. You need to set out and do research on which nutritional discipline is right for you depending on your goal. If you need to lose weight, gain weight, or focus on longevity and reduce inflammation, you need to consume based on your desired outcome - let that be your why and your compass.

This book is not a diet book, so I won't make any recommendations here, but I will recommend a basic framework based on what has already been shared here. I repeat:

- Minimize as much sugar as possible. Not just refined sugar, but all types of sugar. Be aware of pseudo names to disguise sugar, such as corn syrup, nectars, and fructose. If you can cut out processed sugars completely, go for it.

- Cut out gluten and / or processed flours. These have been shown to lead to major inflammation in the body and the brain.

- Cut out seed oils completely. This includes, but is not limited to, grapeseed oil, sunflower oil, canola oil, just to name a few.

- Watch your dairy intake, and only consume the best dairy you can get your hands on. Diary is becoming highly processed like wheat and gluten, leading to further intolerances within the body.

- Minimize, if not completely remove, alcohol. If you're dealing with self doubt, anxiety, or depression in any form, avoid alcohol all together. Not only does it mess with your hormones, but it's a depressant and should be avoided at all costs.

It doesn't matter if you're trying to gain weight for fitness or lose weight for health. The above points are the foundation of any healthy nutritional discipline. As part of your chosen discipline, you need to track your intake, for what you measure you can manage. Using a simple app like MyFitnessPal can help immensely. It has a free version and has an immense library of virtually everything we consume. It breaks down macronutrients, micronutrients, sets calorie parameters, and is a food log. All of this will not only help you manage your intake, but will help keep you motivated and on track.

Moving to movement (see what I did there?). Regarding your movement, this too is up to you. If you're just starting your exercising journey, don't set the goal to go to the gym two hours per day. Start by walking for 10 minutes once a day for a week. Then 10 minutes twice a day for a week. Then, as time progresses, make one of those walks 15 minutes. Then make the other 15 minutes. Continue to grow week over week with the focus on increasing your movement as much and as often as possible.

This principle is the same for all of us. We need to push ourselves week after week to continue to progress. The data shows that your growth should be right around 4%. This push is not a massive one - you should not aim to deadlift 300lbs one week and 400lbs the next, nor should you aim at walking for 10 minutes one week and an hour the next. The goal is to make continual progress, FOREVER.

# THEREFORE, YOU NEED TO ASSESS WHERE YOU ARE NOW AND MAKE MICRO MOVEMENTS IN THE RIGHT DIRECTION - TOWARDS YOUR DESIRED BEING, THE OPTIMAL VERSION OF YOU THAT YOU'VE NAMED TO AIM IN PREVIOUS EXERCISES.

Again, this is not a fitness or exercise book, so I won't make any recommendations here. What I will recommend is that you do a real inventory of where you are and where you want to be. From there, just do a Google search on exercise programs or outlines that fit your parameters. There are countless free programs that will work for you. The newest thing is AI - Chat GPT can write you a plan based on your input. There are no more excuses.

The point of this exercise is to continue to align who you are now with who you desire to become. Continue to clarify the picture of your Optimal Self. Not only do you give him / her a name, but now you're writing a program to get you to that person physically.

THIS IS YOUR OPTIMAL SELF ROAD MAP, AND THE ONLY WAY TO GET TO THAT PERSON IS TO PUT IN THE WORK, TAKE THE STEPS, AND EXECUTE YOUR PLAN TO BECOME THEM. IT'S ALL WITHIN YOUR CONTROL. GRAB THAT TRUTH, CREATE YOUR PLAN, AND EXECUTE.

# CHAPTER 6
## INNER MOUNTAINS OF MASTERY |
## MENTAL & EMOTIONAL
### "DIFFICULTIES STRENGTHEN THE MIND, AS LABOR DOES THE BODY." - SENECA

---

In the other chapters, I share big events that illustrate the potency of the topic at hand. In this chapter, however, the most potent example I can give of the power of mental and emotional tools does not come from one big event, but from thousands of little ones. With respect to our mental and emotional fitness, it's death by paper cuts and shavings make a pile. But only all the time.

We've all got different weight that we carry - parenthood, work, school, family drama, friend drama, view of self, and of course what we're addressing in this book, self-doubt, anxiety, and depression. These things, over time, grind us into a powder. That's just life. But it is up to us to decide which powder we want to become. Do you want to be powdered snow that melts under the heat of pressure? Or do you want to be black powder that has explosive power and propels us forward?

Just like physical challenges, we can hold light weight for a longer period than we can hold heavy weight. But if I asked you to hold a five pound weight out to the side with straight arms, eventually what once seemed light would no longer be so. The weight itself didn't change, but our strength diminished over time, leading to us having to drop our arms and perhaps even the five pound weight itself.

So, too, is our mental and emotional state. Things seem like no big deal at first - they are light and therefore bearable. But over time, they break us down, especially as we allow them to pile on. It is our responsibility to not only bear the weight in a stationary or fixed fashion, but load it up, squat that weight, and grow from it.

This is the difference between a Fixed Mindset and a Growth Mindset[13]. By definition, a Fixed Mindset is one that either is something, or it's not. It's either intelligent, or it's not. It either has a certain talent or ability or it doesn't. It's FIXED in its ways.

# A GROWTH MINDSET, ON THE OTHER HAND, IS ONE THAT REALIZES THAT ITS CURRENT STATE IS SIMPLY A STARTING POINT. ANYTHING THAT IS DESIRED TO BE ACHIEVED, CAN BE ACHIEVED. AND MOST IMPORTANTLY, THE PAIN THAT LIFE FORCES YOU THROUGH IS SIMPLY AN OPPORTUNITY TO LEARN AND GROW.

These two mindsets are opposite sides of the same coin. It is up to us to decide which one we want to live with.

Whatever mental state you're in now, that's your starting point. I don't care how far down you may feel, it's where you must start. After all, the tallest buildings in the world also have the deepest foundations. If you are like I was, you hitting rock bottom and then digging your grave is only laying the foundation upon which you can now build. Great. Now is time to put down the shovel and begin the building process.

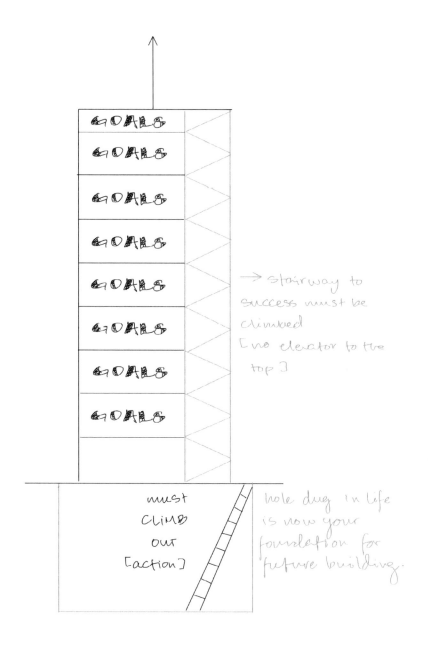

GOALS
GOALS
GOALS
GOALS
GOALS
GOALS
GOALS
GOALS

→ Stairway to success must be climbed [no elevator to the top]

must CLIMB OUT [action]

hole dug in life is now your foundation for future building.

We've discussed this in previous chapters, but life will always happen to you. There will always be pain involved, but there doesn't have to be suffering.

Pain is a physical sensation or signaling indicating an event within the body. This is inevitable. Because of this inevitability, pain should not be fought, but should be embraced. Pain is an outstanding teacher, both of what to do and of what not to do. We learn from it, and it hardens us as the pounding of steel hardens the sword. And while pain is necessary, suffering[14] is a choice.

# SUFFERING IS THE RESISTANCE TO THE REALITY OF WHAT YOU'RE GOING THROUGH. IT'S THE DENIAL, THE DISBELIEF, AND THE UNWILLINGNESS TO ACCEPT REALITY FOR WHAT IT IS. THIS HAPPENS WHEN WE ARE FIXED IN A POSITION IN LIFE, REFUSING TO ACCEPT THE CHANGE THAT LIFE IS FORCING UPON US.

Suffering, unfortunately, is something we choose to put ourselves through. The good news is that it is something that we can remove ourselves from.

To remove suffering from ourselves, we must develop this growth mindset. The first step is to remove the mentality that things shouldn't be how they are. Again, that mentality is fixed. "This shouldn't be happening to me," or "it's not fair that it happened this way," is keeping you in a fixed position in the past. We need to replace that thought process with a growth mindset. "This shouldn't be happening to me," needs to become:

# "WHILE THIS SUCKS AND I DON'T WANT THIS TO BE HAPPENING TO ME, I KNOW I CAN LEARN SOMETHING FROM THIS AND BECOME BETTER FROM IT. I JUST HAVE TO FIND OUT HOW."

This Growth mindset, as the name states, allows us to grow through trials rather than simply go through them.

To G.R.O.W., we have to do what this acronym stands for.

## G.R.O.W. = GET RID OF WOE.

We need to remove this sense of woe is me, life happened to me, and I can't do anything about it. That is the mentality that I had and held onto, and it kept me buried for years. Here is the cold hard truth about life - it's not fair. To life, fair is a four letter f-word. But if you removed yourself from your position for a minute, became a Subjective Spectator, and looked at other people's lives, there will always be hundreds, if not thousands, possibly millions of others in this world that have it worse than you. So what's fair now?

So this has to be our end goal - to develop a mindset that is one of growth. But again, this begs the question of "how?" Let's dive in.

First, we need to recognize that life, unlike school or your job, rewards effort rather than outcomes. Often, our mental state deteriorates because we haven't achieved something. We didn't get the "A" on the exam, or we didn't get the promotion that we wanted. When that happens, we get down on ourselves and our mentality becomes increasingly negative. This is the starting point in climbing the Mental Mountain - realizing that LIFE REWARDS EFFORT, not outcomes.

In today's world, we are increasingly focused on what we have rather than focusing on what it takes to achieve or attain. Life is not about what we have, but what we become. Therefore, the constant obtaining of THINGS does nothing for us in the long run. I'm not saying we can't reward ourselves for our accomplishments. We should absolutely do that. But our mentality should not be determined by the things we obtain, but by the all-out effort that we put forth to attain them. After all, trying to create a good mental headspace by obtaining more stuff is like trying to satisfy your hunger by taping sandwiches on your body. Satisfaction does not come from outside…

This realization is extremely important because, unlike school and work, life does not give the lesson and then provide you with a test. Life throws the test at you and then expects you to learn the lesson. When that is the case, the outcome is not the focal point, but the lesson learned through the experience. To ensure we learn the lesson that life has asked us to learn, we have to shift our mentality to "GROW through" rather than go through, and give it all we have - our 100% effort. From there, the outcome will dictate itself.

I don't believe that there is a better example of this concept of G.R.O.W. through vs go through than our veterans coming back from combat. While we're all familiar with PTS (Post Traumatic Stress), very few of us are familiar with PTG (Post Traumatic Growth).

In a study, "A Resilient Warrior: Coping Positively with Combat Stress Exposure[15]," William Stallard set out to discover why some veterans experience PTS while others experience PTG. His findings are not only applicable to veterans, but to us as regular civilians looking to improve our mental states as we climb the Mental Mountain.

Stallard shared one positive trait found in those who experienced PTG - that being resiliency. He likened resiliency to a "severely wind-blown tree" and the different forms it can take.

- "Recovery - a severely wind-blown tree that bends without braking, and after the winds stops, returns to its original shape.

- Resistance - a tree that appears unaffected by the wind; essentially, it stands strong and does not bend or break under stress.

- Reconfiguration - tree that bends when blown severely over time, and because of the severity and prolonged nature of the wind, changes shape to adapt or accommodate to the effects of stress."

While it's good to know which one of these trees best represents us (I'm number 3, or at least I was) it's also important to know that resiliency, while a growth trait, is a slow growth trait.

The trait that had the best relationship with PTG was what Stallard called "hardiness", or what I'll refer to as Anti-Fragility, coming from Nassim Taleb.

# ANTI-FRAGILITY, AS I DEFINE IT, IS A COMBINATION OF VIRTUES SUCH AS COMMITMENT, CONTROL, AND CHALLENGE ORIENTATION THAT CREATE THE COURAGE AND DISCIPLINE TO TURN POTENTIAL TRAGEDIES INTO GROWTH OPPORTUNITIES.

This is the mindset that we need to strive for to not just go through, but G.R.O.W. through life.

Lucky for us, we've already talked about these points that lead to anti-fragility. Connection to our higher selves. Control over what we control, leading to our decisions becoming our responsibility. And Challenge Orientation is the "try me vs why me" approach to action, realizing that we have the tools to face what's in front of us head on. Putting these things together provides us with the courage and discipline to see life's difficulties as growth opportunities rather than tragedies, or simply brick walls, that are put up to stop us.

Let's talk about the word DISCIPLINE for a minute, since that is one virtue that leads to anti-fragility. We often hear of discipline with self-improvement, but do we really know what it means? Looking at the etymology of the word, DISCIPLINE comes from the root *disciplina*, meaning "learning or knowledge." It also comes from the root word disciple, or "student; one who studies."

# IN THIS CASE, ANTI-FRAGILITY IS ACHIEVED THROUGH DISCIPLINE, OR LEARNING AND STUDYING OURSELVES IN ORDER TO GROW THROUGH POTENTIAL TRAGEDIES.

The anti-fragile mindset is achieved through being disciplined and constantly learning how to better ourselves through the process of life. Again, we've come full circle - disciplined mindset = growth mindset.

In addition to a disciplined mind, we need a disciplined heart, or better said, disciplined feelings. To reiterate, feelings are temporary, so we need to be disciplined in controlling them to avoid making permanent decisions. After all, our emotions and feelings do not have the right to dictate our actions. We should feel all of them, sure, but we should be the ones deciding which ones we decide to act on. Our emotions do not justify actions.

The fastest way to control our emotions is by managing our energy. Our emotions are heightened when our energy is low, mainly because our willpower is decreased. When our energy is low, we resort to our default settings of angry, defensive, knee-jerk reactions. We need to change that. To do that, we must first recognize what causes our energy to be low and understand our personal triggers. Then we must train daily to control our emotional wellbeing.

In the 12-step program, they use an acronym to identify our main triggers.

## THE ACRONYM IS H.A.L.T., AND IT STANDS FOR HUNGRY, ANGRY, LONELY, TIRED. THESE ARE THE FOUR MAIN TRIGGERS THAT EFFECT US EMOTIONALLY, AND IN TURN, CHANGE OUR BEHAVIOR IF LEFT UNCHECKED.

My biggest trigger is tired. Personally, I'm okay with hungry. I've done a five day fast and many other smaller fasts over the years, leading me to train my emotional state while hungry. I can deal with my anger fairly well. Like the Hulk, I'm always a little angry, so I have years of training in that state as well, leading to good control in that state. I do fairly well being lonely. I'm an introvert by nature, so I'm not seeking to be surrounded by others all the time. Over the years, I have fallen in love with solitude - meditation, journaling, and introspection have become great friends of mine. But when I get overly tired, all hell breaks loose. The other letters in the acronym give way. I eat all the crap I know I shouldn't. My anger, along with other emotions, gives way to behavior I KNOW is bad. And when I'm overly tired, I feel as if I'm alone in my endeavors, leaving me to feel isolated and even betrayed by my loved ones. Tired is my biggest trigger. Which of these four triggers can you identify with? Take a second and think about it, identify it, and write it down.

I have realized this pattern over years of paying attention to myself and training under these conditions. Because of this, I now know that tired is my biggest trigger. I know how it presents itself, and I know what to do when it rises to the surface. I know I need to take a step back, become a subjective spectator, and curb any emotions that arise. I know I need to communicate to those around me that I am overly tired and need some personal time to recover, even if it's just 10-15 minutes to meditate or take a quick power nap. I know that when I'm overly tired, I can't make any important decisions. I need to sleep on them, or write them down and come back to them when I'm ready. All of this allows me to remain in control when my emotions begin to run amuck.

Our emotions are directly connected to our energy levels, which are directly connected to our willpower to control them. Think of your energy levels as an emotional battery, much like our beloved cell phones. When our phones drop to 20% or less, we start to panic and search for a way to charge it so it doesn't die on us. We can't bear the thought of being without our phones. We need to have that same approach with ourselves.

WHEN WE HIT THE "LOW BATTERY" MARK WITHIN, WE NEED TO FIND WAYS TO RECHARGE QUICKLY. IF WE DON'T, OUR DECREASED BATTERY LIFE LEADS TO INCREASINGLY HEIGHTENED EMOTIONS, AND THEN AN INCREASE IN POOR DECISION MAKING.

EMOTIONAL BATTERY LEVELS

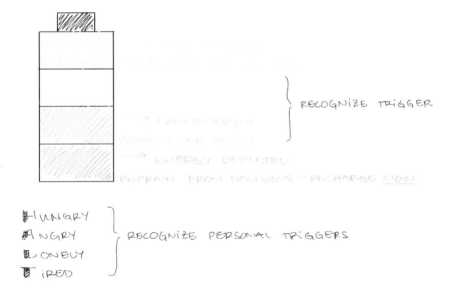

} RECOGNIZE TRIGGER

→ LOW ENERGY
AVOID HARD TASKS

→ ENERGY DEPLETED
REFRAIN FROM DECISIONS · RECHARGE NOW

HUNGRY
ANGRY
LONELY        } RECOGNIZE PERSONAL TRIGGERS
TIRED

All of this, both mental and emotional discipline, needs to be trained. As I mentioned, I know what my trigger is now because I've looked for it. I know how to manage it because I've trained under its conditions. We all need to do the same. This training needs to be done daily. Fortunately, life provides ample opportunities for us to train and learn. We just have to be open to using what life provides us as a training grounds.

# THEN WE HAVE TO JUMP INTO THE ARENA, KNOWING FULL WELL THAT WE'RE GOING TO FAIL, MAKE MISTAKES, AND LOSE SOMETIMES.

That's okay. That is the entire point. Live and learn, as they say.

I call this approach to life's arena as a training ground, "micro-dosing your pain." We need to build mental and emotional calluses, much like we do on our hands. We do that through daily work. Like our hands, we don't want to work them to the bone to where we can't come back the next day and continue our work. Same with our mental and emotional state.

# WE WANT TO MICRO-DOSE OUR PAIN SO THAT WE CAN BREAK DOWN JUST ENOUGH TO LEARN, WHILE PROVIDING US WITH ENOUGH ENERGY TO RECOVER AND COME BACK.

The best way to do this is to develop the Growth Mindset and look for opportunities to train your skills moment to moment to moment. Your partner is bothering you? Great - train your skills.

Your job sucks? Great - train your skills. Your kids are bringing you to your breaking point? Great - train your skills. Buster is beating you to a pulp? Great - recognize your triggers, and train your skills.

Another great way to train your mental and emotional skill set is through physical training. This is why we start with the Physical Mountain. We can use the Physical Mountain as a literal training ground for mental and emotional training. When you climb the Physical Mountain and push yourself, you automatically face the Mental and Emotional Mountains through encountering physical pain. Again, micro-dosing your pain provides you a safe place to train the skills necessary to overcome and optimize.

This approach of micro-dosing pain is critical to long-term success. Why? Simple.

# "WE DON'T RISE TO THE OCCASION, WE FALL TO THE LEVEL OF OUR TRAINING."

If we don't train our minds and hearts to be anti-fragile, they will not become so. Just like everything in life, if we want something, we have to work for it. That work comes as daily mental and emotional exercise. Over time, your level of mental and emotional fitness will increase, your mental and emotional endurance will increase, and you will be able to handle whatever life throws at you, knowing that everything you face is given to you to build you up to the person you're meant to become.

# CHAPTER ACTIVITY
## BREATHE TO REGAIN YOUR CENTER

---

I'd be remiss if I didn't talk about our breathing to regain our mental and emotional control.

## OUR BREATH IS WHAT WE FIRST TAKE WHEN WE COME INTO THIS LIFE, AND IT'S THE LAST THING WE GIVE UP BEFORE WE LEAVE.

Our breath is central to our being, and learning to control it helps us gain control of our mental and emotional status.

While there may be no "right way" to do it, there is definitely a wrong way to do it. And what I mean by there is no right way, I mean that what works for you works for you. But science is clear on the foundation of how breathing should be done, and how it shouldn't be. Namely - don't be a mouth breather.

Our bodies are designed to breathe through the nose. Contrary to what feels right, breathing through your nose actually oxygenates your body better than breathing through your mouth. Furthermore, our noses have great filters to cleanse the air that we breathe, where our mouths don't. For the sake of this book, however, we want to focus on how the body responds to breathing to minimize anxiety and depression.

As we've discussed, our bodies are tightly knit networks that all work together. Our gut affects the brain, which affects the gut, and so on cyclically. Our mind affects the body, and the body affects the mind. Our mind can also affect our breathing, and yes, we also have a cycle here - our breathing can affect the mind. Specifically, our Sympathetic and Parasympathetic Nervous System.

When our body sense that it's in danger, the Sympathetic System is activated, heightening our awareness. With that comes the need to breathe heavily and quickly, leading to mouth breathing. This mouth breathing allows us to get giant amounts of oxygen in at a time, feeding our muscles as we enact our fight, flight, or freeze response. Long story short, we should use mouth breathing only in heightened states of physical stress.

But, again, our bodies don't know the difference in stresses. Running from a bear gets the same response as giving a public speech. This response leads to the same response of mouth breathing, further pushing our sympathetic response. This is what we have to learn to control.

If we have a cyclical response of brain controls breathing, then our breathing should be able to control our brain. And it can. When we recognize which type of state we're in, we can control our response and therefore change the state. Breathing is the best tool to do that.

The best because it's something that works in real time and something you can take with you everywhere you go and deploy at any time. No one is going to question why you're breathing, but they may question why you start punching air if you're trying to fight your way through your nerves…

This is why breathing techniques are taught at the highest levels of performance. From MMA fighters, to First Responders, to Special Operators, breathing is taught to gain control of self in some of the toughest conditions known to man. If breathing can help a sniper stabilize his shot in the midst of a war zone, I'm positive it can help you gain control of your emotions.

Breathing techniques work because they can put you back into a parasympathetic response.

# WHEN WE GAIN CONTROL OF OUR BREATHING, SLOW THINGS DOWN, AND TAKE CONTROL OF OUR SYSTEM WHEN IT'S UNDER PRESSURE, WE MOVE OUT OF THE SYMPATHETIC RESPONSE AND BACK INTO THE PARASYMPATHETIC RESPONSE. THIS ALLOWS US TO THINK MORE CLEARLY, FEEL MORE ACCURATELY, AND THEN ACT MORE DIRECTLY.

There are a couple methods that I'll recommend in a moment, but let's understand the foundation of good breathing first. Number one - everything is through the nose. Number two, inhale is slightly shorter than your exhale, or said the other way, your exhale is slightly longer than your inhale. Number three, breathing should be down into the belly and then into the rest of the diaphragm, not into the chest and then up into the shoulders.

Now that you know the basic rules, let's start with the first recommended breathing technique, which breaks rule number two. This method is known as Box Breathing and is known best for its use in the military to help Operators remain in control while under pressure. As the name indicates, your breathing should form a box - equal on all sides. An example would be: four second inhale, four second hold at the top, four second exhale, four second hold at the bottom. You'd repeat this for a minimum of five breaths, or until you feel like you're in a better state.

Another technique, which is my favorite, is a 6x2x8x2 pattern. Breathe in for six seconds, hold for two, breath out for eight seconds, hold for two. This model, like box breathing, relaxes the body and the mind, allowing you to regain control and reset yourself back to center.

Both methods achieve positive outcomes, such as an increase in energy and focus, a decrease in anxiety and depression, an increase in clarity, and improves future reactions to stress. If you've gotten this far in the book, you know these outcomes are exactly what we're trying to achieve.

When climbing the Mental and Emotional Mountain, proper breathing is critical to our assent.

# LIKE WHEN WE CLIMB THE PHYSICAL MOUNTAIN AND PERFORM PHYSICAL ACTIVITIES, OUR BREATHING SHOULD DICTATE OUR PACE OF ACTION, NOT BE DICTATED BY THE ACTION ITSELF. YOU NEED TO BE THE ONE IN CONTROL, AND THE VERY FIRST THING THAT YOU CAN CONTROL AT ANY TIME IS HOW YOU BREATHE.

The Mental and Emotional Mountains are where most of our energy and willpower is spent. This is because these mountains play across all the others and are the stepping stones to living a higher lifestyle. As we addressed in the Mastery Cycle, our thoughts become our destiny, and they feed off of our emotions. These two Mountains of Mastery are crucial for our wellbeing, and must be mastered if we are to master our lives. If you can't conquer, or at least climb, these mountains consistently, you'll never become Stronger Than Your Pain. But don't let that scare you. Take a deep breath and keep moving forward. You got this.

# CHAPTER 7
## INNER MOUNTAINS OF MASTERY |
## SPIRITUAL & INTUITIONAL
### "ALL THE GODS, ALL THE HEAVENS, ALL THE HELLS ARE WITHIN YOU." - JOSEPH CAMPBELL

---

There was once a beautiful monastery filled with peaceful monks. For years, these monks lived in harmony, celebrating and worshiping their Buddha. The Buddha that they had in the monastery was a massive statue made of pure gold, worthy only of the god they worshipped.

One day, a war was brought to their doorstep. With no thought of their own safety, they rushed to protect and save their Buddha statue. Wondering how they could hide such an enormous statue of gold in such a short time, they realized they had only one choice - they had to cover it. Thinking quickly, they made a plaster from items on hand

and covered this beautiful statue. Within minutes, these monks had covered this statue, making it look like it was made of mud and paper.

As the warriors passed through their village, taking what they wanted and destroying what they didn't, they came across the Buddha statue. They inspected it up and down, concluding that it was nothing more than a simple mud statue. Having some respect for the god, they didn't destroy it, but left it alone as they moved through the rest of the city.

Years went by, turning into decades. Monks continued to live in the monastery after the war, but they had forgotten about this once beautiful statue of their god. It remained covered in mud. Because of this, the monks moved their worship to other, more worthy representations of Buddha.

One day, a group of monks went to move the Buddha. Upon doing so, some of the mud cracked and fell off, revealing the gold that lay hidden underneath. Realizing what they had discovered, they quickly cleaned this statue. As they did, they uncovered a massive statue of their beloved Buddha made of pure gold. It was more glorious than anything else within the monastery, and therefore, was moved to the center of the monastery to be worshiped as the worthy statue it was.

How often do we look at others this way? How often do we view ourselves this way? How often do we see people covered in their outside appearance and deem them unworthy of our attention and affection, not realizing that inside, they are made of pure gold?

We are the same.

# WHILE WE HAVE THESE IMPERFECT REPRESENTATIONS OF WHO WE ARE ON THE OUTSIDE, INSIDE WE ARE ALL PURE GOLD, WORTHY OF EVERYTHING WE DESIRE IN THIS LIFE. IT IS OUR JOB, AND THEREFORE OUR RESPONSIBILITY, TO KNOCK OFF THE MUD THAT IS COVERING US AND LET THE GOLD WITHIN US SHINE.

This chapter is not to discuss religion, but spirituality and intuition. Spirituality in the sense of finding inner peace and purpose. Intuition in trusting our gut feelings that we get from spiritual guidance. After all, we are all spiritual beings living a physical experience.

# THEREFORE, WHILE THE PHYSICAL MOUNTAIN MUST BE CLIMBED FIRST, THE SPIRITUAL MOUNTAIN IS PERHAPS THE MOST IMPORTANT, BECAUSE IT'S WHO WE ARE AT OUR CENTER.

Building on that, why is the Physical Mountain first if the Spiritual Mountain is the most important? To be blunt, the spiritual life is a higher way of living. We can only truly live it when the physical realm of life has achieved a certain level of personal success. Let's break this down.

Imagine a giant archway of spirituality. Once you pass through it, you hit the trailhead to the Inner Mountain of Spirituality. But here's the catch, you have to build the archway in order to pass through. What do you put as the keystone? What is your foundation? What are the pillars composed of? Here's how I view the Archway of Spirituality.

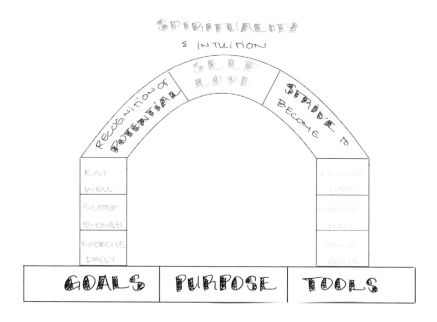

The most important part of any strong archway is the keystone. The keystone bears the weight of the arch and keeps it standing strong. Of course, alongside the keystone are the side stones, or the vous-soirs, that apply the necessary pressure needed to maintain the shape and disperse the pressure the keystone receives. To further support those stones are the pillars, or vertical supports. Each pillar is made of sturdy pieces of stone themselves to ground the weight into the foundation. And then, of course, the solid foundation upon which the archway itself sits.

The keystone of our Spiritual Archway is self-love or self-worth. As we've discussed, self-worth comes from self confidence. How do we gain confidence in ourselves? By doing what we say we will do -

the same way we gain confidence in others. That act, and the actions that proceed it, are achieved on the Physical, Mental, and Emotional Mountains.

This is also where we begin to gain our intuition. Our intuition is the ability to trust our gut feelings. How do we come to trust that? By listening to and acting on what we know to be right and true.

The supporting stones are Recognition of our Potential, along with the daily actions of Striving to Become. As Thomas Edison said, "Vision without execution is just hallucination." We need to act to BECOME the best version of ourselves, not simply visualize. That is done by ascending the Physical Mountain, and now, traversing over to the Spiritual Mountain.

The pillars that support the keystone of Self Love, Recognition, and Striving are made of daily actions. Eat well, sleep enough, and daily exercise, along with the other physical tools we've discussed this far, are one pillar, all of which are experienced on the Physical Mountain. Then we have mindfulness, meditation or prayer, and the sharing of our natural gifts, also known as service. These are all spiritual actions taken as we climb the Spiritual Mountain. Again, all experienced on the other Inner Mountains.

And then we have our foundation upon which we build all of this. This foundation consists of all we have covered this far, but can be summed up in three pieces - our goals (see Chapter 2), our purpose (scattered throughout the book), and our tools to achieve our goals and purpose (entire book). Each one of these further develops our intuition, which our spiritual being can build upon. When we set proper goals and aim to achieve them daily, we climb higher on all the Inner Mountains of Mastery. Eventually, achieving and setting goals leads us to finding a deeper purpose in life, but can only be found higher on these Inner Mountains. How do we climb these Inner Mountains successfully? By deploying our tools moment to moment to moment as needed throughout our journey.

This is why the Physical Mountain must be ascended first before you can successfully begin your ascent up the Spiritual Mountain. You don't have to master the Physical Mountain before you can start your spiritual ascent, but you have to get to a certain point on your physical journey. That point is defined by you and will present itself naturally as you continue your daily climb. In my personal experience, it's somewhere around 90 days of consistent effort. Around this time, I begin to feel a connection to what I am doing and receive a clearer vision as to why I'm doing it.

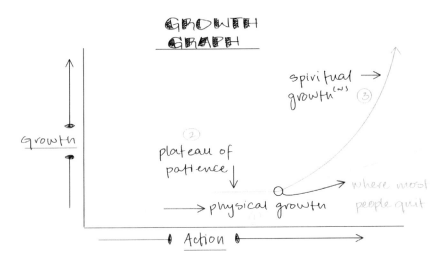

GROWTH GRAPH

: done through physical action

(1) PATIENCE : continued effort physically w/ plateaued results - test how badly you want it

(3) PAYOFF : spiritual growth awakened at exponential growth rate; physical, mental, emotional growth continues

Let's not forget the other Inner Mountains proceeding the Intuitional and Spiritual - the Mental and Emotional Mountains. I have written these chapters in this order for a reason. The Intuitional and Spiritual Mountains are the last focus because in order to truly give ourselves to the higher power of a spiritual life, we have to first make sure that we are deserving of being received.

I'm not saying that we have to be baptized, cleansed, or "worthy" enough in order for this higher life to receive us.

# I AM SAYING THAT JUST LIKE IN ANY RELATIONSHIP, WE HAVE TO BE STEADY ENOUGH IN OUR OWN LIVES IN ORDER TO BE WELCOMED BY THOSE AROUND US.

If I don't take care of myself, eat poorly, am sluggish and sloth-like, constantly have emotional and mental explosions, lose my temper, give into every temptation that is placed in front of me, constantly focus on the negative, and neglect any personal growth (as I once was during my lowest years), am I going to be accepted by those around me? I sure hope not! We know we become those we surround ourselves with, so no one should allow that person into their lives. Trying to live the spiritual life is the same.

# WE CANNOT NEGLECT OUR FOUNDATION OF PHYSICAL, MENTAL, AND EMOTIONAL WELLBEING AND SIMULTANEOUSLY HAVE THE ABILITY TO TRUST OURSELVES WHILE WE STRIVE TO BE A SPIRITUAL BEING.

It's against the laws of nature and simply won't work. Life, God, The Universe - call it whatever you want - will not accept us no matter how hard we try, because we are not ready for it. All of this is tied together and must coexist if we are to reach our highest potential.

If we are to enter heaven, receive enlightenment, or be rein-carnated into a better person rather than a cockroach, we have to act according to that outcome. Just as every religion has its rules and commandments, so, too, does life in general. What we put into this world is what we get out of it. That implies that we must first insert our input before we are given our desired output.

This brings us to HELL, literally. This has brought us to the topic of hell, but the above statement is what ACTUALLY brings us to hell. Again, removing religion and focusing purely on the spiritual, hell is not a destination of fire and brimstone that is only realized at the end of our lives. No. Hell is much more than that and it is ever present in our daily lives.

# HELL IS WHEN WE VISUALIZE OURSELVES LAYING ON OUR DEATHBED AND WE COME FACE TO FACE WITH THE PERSON WE COULD HAVE BECOME, YET DIDN'T. HELL, THEREFORE, IS THE DAILY EXPERIENCE OF NOT CLOSING THE GAP BETWEEN WHO WE ARE NOW AND WHO WE ARE CAPABLE OF BECOMING.

If we are not moving forward, we are moving backwards - there is no such thing as a stagnant being. So if we are not moving forward towards becoming who we're meant to be, we are moving away from that, and that, my friend, is as real as hell gets.

That then leads us to question how, from a spiritual standpoint, we can avoid hell. Great question. And as we've discussed, closing the gap between current you and potential you have to be done across the other Inner Mountains. Our daily actions lead to our destiny: thoughts, words, and ACTIONS. No more needs to be mentioned there. But when we approach the spiritual, it is the same format. Daily action towards your potential being. This, at least to me, is the purest form of prayer.

## IF GOD IS CONSTANTLY FOUND ATOP MOUNTAINS, DOES OUR EFFORT TO ASCEND THE INNER MOUNTAINS OF MASTERY NOT BRING US FACE TO FACE WITH GOD AND ALLOW US TO STAND WORTHILY BEFORE HIM?

The spiritual actions, I think, are the hardest ones to do because they are fairly ambiguous in their nature. How do you measure spirituality? It's a hard question to answer. Therefore, our actions must be targeted and trackable, just like all our actions.

Spiritual actions consist mainly of actions that are directed inward. Meditation, prayer, journaling, visualization, and asking deep questions of yourself.

## THE MOST DIFFICULT PART, HOWEVER, COMES FROM HAVING TO SEPARATE YOURSELF FROM THE CURRENT LIFE YOU'RE LIVING IN ORDER TO SEE WHICH LIFE YOU ARE CAPABLE OF LIVING.

To gain that perspective, one must have great intuition into personal possibilities. Let's dive in to some specific work to help with that.

Let's first talk about meditation. The studies are clear that this is one of the best ways to unlock spiritual potential. As Marcus Aurelius said, "Nowhere can man find a quieter or more untroubled retreat than in his own soul." When we talk about separating yourself from the world around you to find your true potential, this is how it's done. We must go to our inner world to escape the outer world.

We can do meditation in many forms, so pick which one works best for you. I'm not going to go into detail here about all the methods, but true to form here, keep it high level so you can build your foundation.

Many people believe, including myself when I started, that meditation has to be the complete absence of thought. When a thought arises, you fail and have to start over. Simply put - NOPE. Not the case. Meditation is simply an art of being WITH your thoughts, not trying to shut them off.

Find a quiet place to sit with your spine straight. Close your eyes, find a breathing rhythm that works for you. Go back to our breathing exercises from the last chapter. From here, focus on your breath. Count your ins, count your outs. Then begin to recognize what thoughts arise. As they do, don't freak out. Instead, acknowledge them, take a mental note of where your inner dialogue is going, and then return to counting your breaths.

With meditation, as with almost everything in life, there is no failure, only learning. This is the foundation of personal discipline - always a student of self. Meditation is a tool that you can use to learn to quiet the world around you to better listen to your gut and soul.

# THE UNIVERSE, THE SPIRIT, DOES NOT RAISE ITS VOICE SO THAT YOU CAN HEAR IT BETTER AMONG THE SURROUNDING CHAOS. IT SPEAKS IN THE SAME VOLUME - CALM AND QUIET. BECAUSE OF THAT, IF YOU WISH TO HEAR IT, YOU MUST QUIET YOURSELF AND THE WORLD AROUND YOU. THAT IS MEDITATION AT ITS CORE.

This tool allows you to take control of the first part of the Mastery Cycle - controlling your thoughts. As they arise during your practice, acknowledge, and then create space by returning to your breath. As you practice this during meditation, you gain greater abilities to do the same thing in life. Meditation becomes your training grounds for thought control, so when you are in the battle of life, you are ready. Just as we are to micro-dose our physical pain to experience physical growth, we too must micro-dose our spiritual pain to experience spiritual growth.

## "A WARRIOR WINS IN HIS MIND BEFORE HE WINS ON THE BATTLEFIELD." THIS IS THE POWER OF MEDITATION.

The other daily tool that is extremely powerful is journaling. Paired with meditation, your ability to visualize who you want to become grows exponentially.

Again, there are many forms of journaling, so find which way works best for you. As we try to find ourselves, our purpose, and who we're capable of being, I have found that the best form of journaling is virtue journaling. Virtue journaling is something I learned during my HEROIC Certification, and completely changed my perspective on the art. Prior to this, my approach to journaling was, "dear diary," which was never helpful for me. Now, virtue journaling is one of my greatest tools.

This form of journaling is simple and quick. It is broken down into three main parts, each with three subparts. It looks like this:

1. Energy:
    a. Identity:
    b. Virtues:
    c. Behavior:

2. Work:
    a. Identity:
    b. Virtues:
    c. Behavior:

3. Love:
    a. Identity:
    b. Virtues
    c. Behavior:

This comes from the psychologist Sigmund Freud who said that our personal identities are made of two main parts - our work and our love. The energy is added because without good energy (as we address in the previous mountains) we cannot work or love to our fullest potential.

# VIRTUE JOURNALING FORCES YOU TO FOCUS ON WHO YOU DESIRE TO BECOME, WHICH VIRTUES IT TAKES TO LIVE THAT LIFESTYLE, AND THEN THE CHERRY ON TOP, WHICH ACTIONS YOU MUST TAKE TODAY TO LIVE AND ACHIEVE IT.

Over time, this cements itself within you, forcing you to recognize that in order to become, you must visualize and act EVERY SINGLE DAY. As you reflect nightly on how you lived up to those identities, virtues, and behaviors daily, you will close the gap between the current version of you and the desired, optimal version of you. This, just like the other mountains, is how you ascend the intuitional and spiritual ones.

As an example of how this looks in practice, here is my virtue journal in a snapshot:

ENERGY : WARRIOR
VIRTUES: DISCIPLINED, FOCUSED, GRIT, STILL,
CONFIDENT, INTENTIONAL, CONSISTENT
BEHAVIOR: LIFESTYLE PROGRAM [ EAT, MOVE, SLEEP,
JOURNAL, WRITE, LEARN, MEDITATE, DIGITAL SUNSET ]

WORK : LEADER
VIRTUES: EMPATHETIC, OPEN MINDED, DECISIVE,
ENERGIZED, BOLD, PROACTIVE, GOOD LISTENER
BEHAVIOR: DEEP WORK TIME BLOCKS, W·I·N·
[ WHAT'S IMPORTANT NOW ]

LOVE : PARTNER [ AS IN "BATTLE BUDDY" ]
VIRTUES: PATIENCE, KIND, PASSIONATE, CHARITABLE,
HELPFUL, FAITHFUL, SOFT, DISCIPLINED, OUTGOING
BEHAVIOR:
  · WIFE: SERVICE, GOOD LISTENER, PASSIONATE
  · DAUGHTER: SILLY, SOFT, PLAYFUL
  · DAUGHTER: KIND, FORGIVING, TRUST
  · DAUGHTER: FACE-TIME & SMILES

Journaling, in whichever format you choose, allows you to begin the process of becoming the author of your own life. As we've discussed throughout the book, we need to be the one at the center of our Mastery Cycle in order to drive it in the direction we desire. To do that, we have to avoid becoming an individu-ALL, and become an individual with our own goals, purpose, and identity. All of this is to say we need to be our authentic self.

Here's the cool thing about being the author of your life. If we address the etymology of "author", we find this:

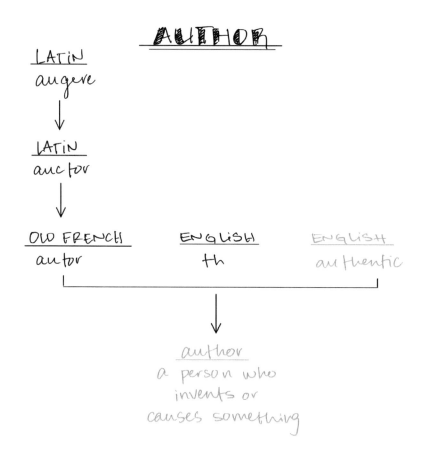

# THIS SHOWS US THAT AUTHOR = AUTHENTIC. IF WE ARE TO BE THE AUTHORS OF OUR LIVES, WE MUST BE THE AUTHENTIC VERSION OF OURSELVES. IF WE ARE TO BECOME THE AUTHENTIC VERSION OF OURSELVES, WE MUST BE THE AUTHOR OF OUR LIVES.

What a beautiful representation of "control the controllables" to determine your outcome.

Journaling helps us become the author of our lives by writing who we desire to become. It allows us to visualize who we are within and then direct us on the actions we need to take to become that person. It gives us insight into our souls and our spirits and allows us to strive towards that being within this physical experience. If we are to advance our lives to this higher level, journaling is a must.

This journaling and meditation combination allows us to spend more time within the gut and soul. As Michael Beckwith calls it[16]:

# WE SPEND MORE TIME ON THE INNER-NET AND LESS TIME ON THE INTERNET.

In today's world, this too is a must. If we are to become the highest version of ourselves, become true individuals, and discover our purpose and what we're capable of, we have to shut off the internet and the flow of consciousness it dictates for us. We need to spend more time within dictating our own direction of flow and consciousness. This is the only way that we can begin to close the gap between who we are now and who we're capable of becoming, avoiding the daily hell of regression.

In addition to journaling and meditation, or better yet, in further combination with the two, we need to ask ourselves the big questions that only spiritual answers can provide answers to. "Where do I come from?" "Why am I here?" "What happens after I die?" "What does the highest version of life look like to me?" "Why does it look that way?"

# THESE QUESTIONS CAN ONLY BE ANSWERED BY STUDYING LIFE AND YOUR PLACE IN IT, ALONG WITH STUDYING YOURSELF AND LIFE'S PLACE WITHIN YOU.

We are spiritual beings have a physical experience. How, then, do you need to bridge the gap physically in order to live up to your personal definition of spirituality?

Finally, we come to prayer. Where meditation is the listening portion of our spiritual conversation, prayer is the talking and asking part. Prayer does not have to be directed towards God. I realize that not everyone believes in God. That's fine. But we must recognize that there is a higher power in life that is listening to our needs and determining if we're worthy of receiving answers based on our actions.

As we begin to ask these larger questions of ourselves, we can then turn to life, God, the universe, and ask these questions. It's when we give these questions and the outcomes over to this higher power that we begin to truly let go of the physical and realize the spiritual.

# WHATEVER HAPPENS IS MEANT TO HAPPEN. WE CANNOT CONTROL THAT FLOW OF LIFE, THEREFORE WE MUST LEAVE THE UNCONTROLLABLES TO THE HIGHER POWER THAT IS LIFE ITSELF. WE THEN FOCUS OUR ENERGY ON OUR ACTIONS, CONSTANTLY DRIVING TOWARDS WHAT WE CAN CONTROL, REALIZING THAT THE ONLY TRUE CONTROLLABLE IN LIFE IS WHO WE ARE IN THIS MOMENT.

The rest is not up to you. We are specks of dust living on a giant space rock that is hurtling through space at thousands of miles per hour, circling a ball of fiery-hot gas that is also flying through space with destination unknown as we expand into endless nothingness. To think that our small "life problems" will affect that somehow is insane. There is so much out of our control - we need to let it go. The sooner we realize that, turn it over to the higher power in life, and accept that as it is, the sooner we find peace and discipline in our lives.

As we realize our spiritual being is the end goal, the physical, mental, and emotional all fall into place as simply means to that end. The means of teaching us lessons to become better humans in order to live the end result as a spiritual being. That, in the end, is life.

# ALL WE CAN HOPE FOR IS THAT WE LEARN ALL THAT WE CAN SO THAT WHEN WE PASS ON, WE LEAVE BEHIND A MARK THAT CAN CHANGE THE WORLD FOR THE BETTER, AND LIVE ON LONG AFTER WE DIE.

# CHAPTER ACTIVITY
## DEFINE YOUR PERSONAL CODE OF CONDUCT

---

This chapter activity is the last activity in the book and is so for a reason. It's difficult. It's time consuming. And the goal is to define who you are, what you believe in, and what you stand for. This activity is to define and create your own Life Values and Code of Conduct.

I have provided an example of my Code of Conduct that I created with the support and approval of my wife and, eventually, my children. This Code of Conduct is the foundation upon which you stand in this life. It is where you root your being. It defines what you believe and how you live so that when life throws the inevitable curve ball, you can stand firm at the plate and continue swinging. We all need our own code if we are to withstand the barrage of life's pitches.

To create your code will take all the previous chapter exercises coming together. You'll need to know the value of your thoughts, the power of your words - internally and externally - and the importance of your actions and inaction. You'll need to define the best version of you. You'll need to ask the 100 questions of yourself and answer them, at least your top 10. You'll need to create a mantra that you can live by - one that embodies your code in a single phrase. You'll need to write a letter from the future you telling you who you need to be, and just as important, who you need to avoid becoming. You'll need to define the importance of your Physical Inner Mountain and how you plan to climb it daily. You'll have to understand how to re-center yourself in times of trial, grasping hold of your Inner Mental and Emotional Mountains. Of course, you'll need to climb those mountains daily. When you do these activities, and truly seek for answers deep within yourself, your Life Values and Code of Conduct will almost write itself.

As you go through these activities, take them seriously and ponder them deeply. Keep a notebook with you and write whatever comes to mind. Recognize what comes to the surface. You'll most likely remember lessons you were taught as a child or lessons you are currently teaching to your own children, family, or friends. It's possible that you'll remember trials you went through and overcame. You may even remember loss, letdown, failures, and low points, while simultaneously recognizing that your existence is proof of your strength and ability to overcome. With all of that in mind, write what you did, thought, and said to overcome those trials that made you who you are today.

While you remember and recognize what you did to overcome, also realize who you desire to become through optimizing your being.

# WHAT DO YOU STRIVE FOR? WHY DO YOU STRIVE FOR THAT? WHO IS CARED FOR AS YOU BECOME A BETTER PERSON? WHO AND WHAT DO YOU LEAVE BEHIND AS YOU STRIVE FOR PERSONAL MASTERY?

This Code of Conduct is your proof that you've overcome and that you are constantly optimizing YOU through your daily ACTIONS. You should write all of this out, print it, and place it where you can see it every day. This code should embody your personal philosophy and direct you in all aspects of your life.

A good exercise to help you get started is to think about this:

# IF YOU WERE TO LEAVE THIS WORLD, WHAT WOULD YOU LEAVE BEHIND TO HELP IT REMEMBER YOU AS YOU WANT TO BE REMEMBERED?

If you could write a single page that would reflect who you are, what you believe in, and how you lived your life so people would remember your legacy, what would you write? THAT is your Code of Conduct.

To help you, I have shared mine below. Feel free to use mine as a template. "A candle loses nothing by lighting another candle." Let this candle that provides me light in the darkness provide you with any light that you may need.

# THE WASSOM'S
## Life Values and Code of Conduct

THESE ARE NOT COMMANDMENTS SET IN STONE. RATHER, THESE ARE A FEW GUIDELINES TO HELP YOU DEVELOP YOUR OWN ETERNAL VALUES AND CODE. WE INVITE YOU TO QUESTION, REFUTE, CHANGE, AND RE-WRITE ANY OF THESE VALUE POINTS AS YOU SEE APPROPRIATE TO BETTER FIT YOUR LIFE'S UNIQUE PATH, AS LONG AS THE CHANGES YOU MAKE LEAD TO GREATER PERSONAL GROWTH AND NOT PERSONAL DETERIORATION.

- Family come first. PERIOD. Who becomes your family is your choice, but blood is family for time and eternity.

- We care more about what shines INSIDE than what shines OUTSIDE. This goes for ourselves and others.

- We do not focus on the successes or failures of yesterday. We focus on TODAY and create a brighter future by making the best of what is present here and now.

- We earn what we obtain – especially TRUST and RESPECT. We also recognize that all we've earned can be lost with one wrong decision.

- We are driven by ETHOS – our ethos, not the ethos of others. Doing what is RIGHT precedes all other benefits.

- We strive for balance and growth in all things – Spiritual, Emotional, Physical, Mental, and Intuitional; in this we focus on the journey, not the end, for there is no end to growth.

- We believe that very little is needed to make a happy life; it is all within yourself and in your way of thinking.

- We believe "the more we SWEAT in times of peace, the less we BLEED in times of war." Consistent preparation is the foundation to success.

- We do not wait to react, but are proactive in our decisions and act with tactful precision based on our desired outcome.

- We NEVER quit, especially when times get hard. Instead, we square up and address our obstacles head on.

- We are ACCEPTING and TOLERANT to everyone and their situation. We are happy for those who are happy.

- We are DISCIPLINED in our lifestyle. We become disciples of something bigger than ourselves – whatever that may be.

- We develop excellence as a HABIT, not just a characteristic. Excellence is part of who we are.

- We LEAD in all that we do, yet we are ready to be led by others when necessary.

- We are committed to SELF MASTERY. We have power over our minds, not outside events. This is where we find our strength.

- We are always seeking to learn new things and are open to learn from anyone who is willing to teach.

- We believe that FAILING at something does not make you a failure, but is merely an opportunity to learn and grow.

- We seek after good things, regardless of the source. We do not judge what is good based on the messenger.

- We take full RESPONSIBILITY for our choices and the consequences. Placing blame in unacceptable.

- We are OPTIMISTIC, especially in times of DARKNESS. We recognize that it's not what happens to you, but how you react that matters.

- We are PROUD of who we are. We do not respond to what others think about us and we remember that our character is something worth protecting.

- We are the first to FORGIVE, but we do not make the same mistake twice.

- We do not do common. MEDIOCRITY is unacceptable and unsettling in our lifestyles.

- We do all we can to avoid war, but if the time comes to fight, we are first in, last out, and do not accept defeat.

# YOU ARE CAPABLE OF INFINITE GREATNESS, BUT IT IS UP TO YOU TO RECOGNIZE THAT AND STRIVE TO ACHIEVE IT DAILY.

As someone who has hit rock bottom, dug my grave, tried to lie in it, and fortunately, was lifted out, I can promise you that you have the ability to overcome and optimize and live this higher lifestyle that you are seeking. The terrifying, yet absolutely liberating, fact is - it's all on you.

# YOU'RE STRONGER THAN YOUR PAIN. YOU CAN DO THIS. BELIEVE THAT FIRST. AND THEN GO PROVE YOURSELF RIGHT. EVERY. SINGLE. DAY.

# SECTION 2 SNAPSHOT
## PUTTING IT ALL TOGETHER

# INNER MOUNTAINS OF MASTERY

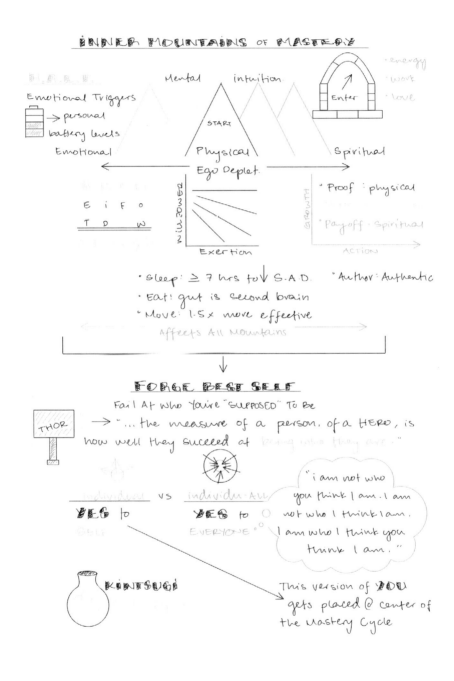

H.A.L.T.

Emotional Triggers
→ personal
battery levels
Emotional

Mental      Intuition

• energy
• work
• love
Enter

START

Physical
Ego Deplet.

Spiritual

E  i  F  o
T  D   W

IN POWER

Exertion

GROWTH

• Proof : physical

• Payoff : spiritual

ACTION

• Sleep: ≥ 7 hrs to ↓ S.A.D.       • Author : Authentic
• Eat: gut is second brain
• Move: 1.5x more effective

Affects All Mountains

↓

# FORGE BEST SELF

Fail At who You're "SUPPOSED" To Be

THOR

→ "... the measure of a person, of a HERO, is
how well they succeed at being who they are."

individual  VS  individu-ALL

YES to          YES to O
                EVERYONE °°

"i am not who
you think i am. i am
not who i think i am.
i am who i think you
think i am."

KINTSUGI

This version of YOU
gets placed @ center of
the Mastery Cycle

# CHAPTER 8
## PROCESS PROVES OUTCOMES

**"I WAS IN DARKNESS, BUT I TOOK THREE STEPS AND FOUND MYSELF IN PARADISE. THE FIRST STEP WAS A GOOD THOUGHT, THE SECOND A GOOD WORD, AND THE THIRD, A GOOD DEED." - FRIEDRICH NIETZSCHE**

---

This book not only outlines some tools that you can use to overcome and optimize, but it shares many key tools that I have used over the last 15 years, and still use to this day, to become stronger than my pain.

To this day, I still deal with self-doubt, anxiety, and depression. Buster still busts my chops on almost a daily basis. I still doubt my capabilities at work, as a writer, as a creator, as a husband, as a father, as an athlete - the list goes on. But now that I not only know these tools, but apply them daily, I can continue forward regardless of that doubt. How? Because I have come to trust myself and my capabilities.

So while I may have doubt for a moment, I attribute that to Buster, push him out, converse with my best self in Alexander Wolfe, high five my current self, and get back on track to becoming who I know I'm capable of becoming.

With these tools, you can do the same thing. But, you have to do more than just know, you have to put that knowledge into action.

## AFTER ALL, KNOWLEDGE IS POWER, BUT ONLY WHEN APPLIED.

Otherwise, it's simply unused data, and there is no power in that.

Learning how to apply these tools is a constant process. You won't try one day and wake up the next day feeling better. I wish it worked like that. But, truthfully, we must apply these tools daily. Why? Because as soon as you stop moving forward, you start sliding backward.

I know this to be true for me. If I don't track, I slack. If I don't manage my workout plan and schedule, track my macros with an app, and watch my sleep time and wake up time, I neglect them and soon find myself depressed and anxious, doubting my capabilities to take on life's challenges. If I don't meditate, journal, and visualize who I want to become, I lose sight of that person and fall backward into my default setting. And, unfortunately for me, I don't have a very good default setting. If I don't actively practice taking care of myself, my self-love and self-worth quickly diminishes because naturally I don't deem myself worthy of being taken care of, and my lack of action confirms that.

# ALL OF THIS SAID, WE MUST ACT DAILY - MOMENT TO MOMENT TO MOMENT TO OVERCOME OURSELVES IF WE WANT TO OPTIMIZE OUR POTENTIAL AND TRULY BECOME STRONGER THAN OUR PAIN.

Closing out the opening chapter that was filled with pain, personal torture, and a near suicidal experience, I want to express how grateful I am for life now.

Starting with my poem - DEATH - I finally found closure. When I originally wrote this, it hung over me like a dark cloud. It had no closure for years, and neither did I. I wrote the first half when I was 11, and only finished the second half while writing this book at 32. That is how long some of these processes take. But that's okay. Looking at an acronym for H.O.P.E., this finally came to fruition - Hold On, Pain Ends. This pain of my grandmother's passing finally ended 16 years later. The poem now finishes like this:

Death is a very scary thing.

You feel like you have lost your wings.

You feel like you could die of pain.

It's all your fault and all your blame.

When someone dies you can't go on.

You feel just like your heart has gone.

You feel like you could be alone.

You can only speak in monotone.


You don't know what to do or say.

You sit in the corner of a room all day.

You feel like you're in great despair.

You can't do anything but sit and stare.


**BUT NOW I KNOW THAT THERE IS MORE,
AND DEATH IS NOT THE FINAL DOOR.
LIFE CONTINUES TO LIVE ON,
EVEN AFTER SOMEONE'S GONE.**


**RATHER THAN BE MAD AND SCARED,
BE GRATEFUL FOR THE TIME YOU SHARED.
FOR TIME ON EARTH IS SHORT AND SWEET,
BUT HEAVEN, AN ETERNAL TREAT.**

# THE STING OF DEATH IS PRESENT STILL, OCCASIONALLY THE HEART IS ILL. BUT CLOSURE, NOW, IS WHAT REMAINS. HERE NOW LOVE, AND GONE ARE PAINS.

Even reading this now, I tear up. Now, however, my tears are of gratitude and peace rather than despair and hatred. I finally, after years of fighting, have found closure.

To add to the closure that came with me finishing the poem, my dad, who I'll get to in a minute, shared a note that my grandmother wrote to me on the back of my poem. She said:

# "MY DEAREST GRANDSON, THIS IS VERY PROFOUND FOR ONE SO YOUNG. WHEN MY TIME COMES TO LEAVE THIS EARTH, PLEASE DO NOT SIT IN A CORNER ALL DAY. PLEASE CELEBRATE WITH AND FOR ME THAT I AM IN HEAVEN WITH MY HEAVENLY FATHER, SINGING WITH THE CHOIR."

This has helped me realize that while I miss her, I need to live a life worthy of her memory. I did not live up to that wish of hers for years. But today, and all the days ahead of me, I strive to.

---

Regarding my parents, who at the start of all of this were my enemies, are now some of my best friends. While they could have done things better during my hard times, I have realized that I am responsible for the misery that I put myself through. I am also, in my opinion, largely responsible for the misery that I put them through.

I have learned through the years that, as I have shared in this book, that life is going to happen, and while I can't control that, I can control my reaction to it. I didn't do that well during those years. In fact, I played the victim. I acted as if it hurt me the most, when there was no way that could be true. It was my father's mother, after all, and he accepted it for what it was - part of life. He was hurt, of course. He was mad that she was ripped from him and the family 20+ years too early. He was sad whenever he thought about everything he wouldn't be able to share with her as time went on. But like the good man that he is, he accepted it for what it was. A tragedy that was meant to be born well. I have learned from his example and try to do the same myself now.

I have also come to realize that my mom was my first Stoic Philosopher. I didn't realize it until I officially began studying the philosophy and seeking after something greater than myself. My mom was, and still is, a Stoic. She has wisdom beyond her years and love is her super power. I see it in how she helps my wife and me raise our children, and I cannot help but tear up with appreciation as I see her pour her wisdom out for them. As she does so, I learn more and more what it is to be a good, involved parent. What she does for my children gives me great insight into what she did (and still does) for me.

I have never known true love until I became a parent. With this newfound perspective, I am beyond grateful for all that my parents did for me during those torturous years I put them through, and simultaneously embarrassed and ashamed of who I was. It is this recognition of who I once was and who I am still capable of becoming if I don't use these tools daily that keeps the fire lit within my soul to constantly improve. I know who I can be, both for the positive and the negative, and I refuse to become the savage victim I once was.

Because of this new perspective, I now know my worth. I am proud of who I have become and what I have overcome. I am excited about the future rather than dreading its presence. I now derive my worth from me rather than from those around me. I finally feel like I am my own individual, rather than the cumulative individu-ALL that I once was. Most importantly, I now know that I am worth healing, caring for, and protecting.

I have found a grand purpose and passion for this work. I have learned the value of having the strength for you become the strength for two. Getting married to my high school sweetheart, I realize I must be strong enough to take care of me if I am to be strong enough to take care of her. Being a father to three beautiful and wonderful daughters, I realize that my strength must be derived in deep purpose if I am to raise them with the skills they need to not only survive, but thrive in this world, as my parents did with their children.

# I REALIZE I CAN'T HAVE A MESSAGE WITHOUT A MESS, AND THAT I NEED TO SHARE THAT MESS WITH THE WORLD AND USE IT AS MY SUPERPOWER.

All of this has taken years of repetitive study and practice. And while I feel like I am finally in a good place, I know that the second I stop, all the success will stop, too.

That is why this chapter is called "Process Proves Outcomes." I did not simply focus on being better, and then it happened. I did not simply want to be a good husband, and then it happened. I did not simply wish to be a good father, and then it happened. I had to figure out what the process was and then live that process daily. Only then could I make progress towards improvement. Over time, that progress derived from the process will determine the outcome.

# WE HAVE TO LET THE OUTCOME BECOME AN ORGANIC BYPRODUCT OF THE PROCESS.

We must use these tools shared in this book daily and as needed if we are to overcome and optimize our potential. You don't become Stronger Than Your Pain by focusing on the desire to become so, you become Stronger Than Your Pain by living as necessary on a daily basis. You develop your mantra, control your thoughts, speak to yourself as you would a loved one, act according to what you know is best, not simply how you feel in the moment. You must take care of yourself physically if you are to take care of yourself mentally, emotionally, and spiritually. You must learn to breathe and take control of the space between stimulus and response. You must separate yourself from your negativity and aim yourself towards your highest potential. You must ask yourself big questions and seek to answer them personally. And here's the kicker - you have to do it daily, FOREVER.

# THE WORK IS NEVER DONE. YOU ARE OWED NOTHING. IF YOU WANT SOMETHING OUT OF THIS WORLD, YOU BETTER BE PREPARED TO PUT SOMETHING INTO THIS WORLD FIRST, AND THAT HAS TO BE YOUR 100% EFFORT, WHATEVER THAT MEANS FOR YOU. YOU GET OUT WHAT YOU PUT IN, NOT WHAT YOU THINK YOU DESERVE.

So if you're in a place that you don't want to be in, wishing your way out won't work. You must put the shovel down, build yourself a ladder, and start climbing each rung until you get out. No one can do it for you.

As we started, we'll finish - I know this sounds terrifying, but when you accept this truth of "it's all on you," you're finally free. You realize you are truly in control of your life. You have the ability to choose your perspective and whether or not you become the victim OF life or the victor OVER it. While we can't control what life throws at us, we can decide how we're going to react to it. Whether we're going to stand at the box and keep swinging, even if we take strike after strike, or we're going to hold back and not even attempt to swing in fear of what those strikes may mean to us. Don't be like I was in my late teens and early twenties, afraid to swing in fear that I'd miss. Always have the courage to swing as hard as you can. Just once, you may hit that home run.

This belief system has become so important to me that I have tattooed pieces of it on me. THE ONE YOU FEED is tattooed on my shoulder, constantly reminding of the mentality that I need to succeed. That I must be the one who feeds the Good Wolf or the Evil Wolf, and that the feeding by me is a choice I get to make. The mantra of STRONGER THAN YOUR PAIN is tattooed on me to remind me that I am capable of anything as long as I believe I am. Life can rear its ugly head at me, but I will not cower and run from it. I am stronger and will face it head on. That is how I choose to live my life.

I didn't have the tools I needed to live a good life 16 years ago. As soon as I realized that, I had found my starting point. I knew at the time that I was not anywhere close to who I wanted to be, and that the only way to get there was one step at a time. The best part of this journey is that there is no end in sight. Who I am today is simply another starting point towards who I am capable of becoming.

# WE MUST TAKE EACH DAY AT A TIME. PAY OUR DUES FOR THE DAY WE'RE IN, FOR THAT IS ALL THAT WE HAVE. TOMORROW IS NEVER PROMISED, SO WE MUST TAKE FULL ADVANTAGE OF THIS MOMENT, ALWAYS STRIVING TO BECOME THE BEST VERSION OF OURSELVES, CLOSING THE GAP BETWEEN WHO WE ARE NOW AND WHO WE'RE CAPABLE OF BECOMING.

This mentality is a process. Using these tools is a daily practice. But as you develop them day by day, your outcome of closing that gap will organically begin to occur. Let your efforts be enough to continue to drive you forward. Let the journey be what satisfies you. Let the stumbles along the way teach you and humble you. Let the victories motivate and fuel you. Let the friends you make along the journey support you. Let the friends you lose along the journey go. Let the bridges you cross stay up in case you, or someone else, need to cross them in the future. Overall, let life play out, and be grateful that you get to have a part in this game. Play it with all that you have and all that you are.

# WHILE YOU MAY NOT BE TODAY, ONE DAY, YOU WILL BECOME STRONGER THAN YOUR PAIN.

/AW/

# BOOK SNAPSHOT
## PUTTING IT ALL TOGETHER

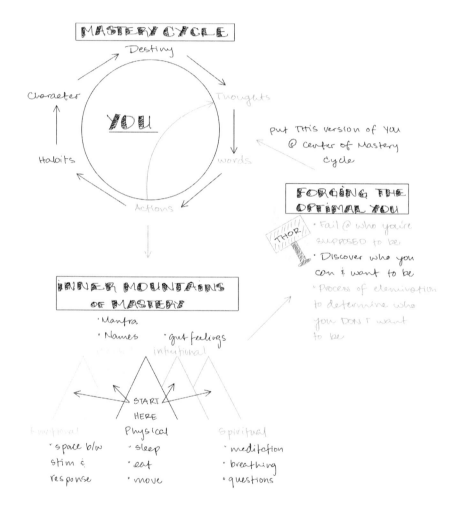

MASTERY CYCLE

Destiny

Character

YOU

Thoughts

Habits

words

Actions

put this version of You
@ center of Mastery
cycle

FORGING THE
OPTIMAL YOU

THOR

• Fail @ who you're
SUPPOSED to be
• Discover who you
can & want to be
• Process of elimination
to determine who
you DON'T want
to be

INNER MOUNTAINS
OF MASTERY

• Mantra
• Names          • gut feelings
                intuitional

START
HERE
Physical
Emotional
• space b/w      • sleep        Spiritual
stim &           • eat          • meditation
response         • move         • breathing
                                • questions

# ACKNOWLEDGMENTS

There is no such thing as a self-made man. In the same light, I may be the author of this book, but I couldn't have done it without a team of people behind and beside me.

Ashley, my love, thank you for always putting up with me. Early mornings, late nights, foregone weekends and missed vacations are just some of the things I bring to the table, and yet you never complain. You are always there to support me, my dreams, and the vision I have for our family. You are my world and everything in it. I not only wouldn't have been able to write this book without your support, but I wouldn't have made it through this life without you. For those big things, and the infinite number of small things on a daily basis, I am forever grateful and indebted to you.

Olivia, Evelyn, and Violet. You don't understand this yet, but you're my reason for being. Everything that your mother and I do we do for you. We love you so much. I am so grateful that I have been blessed with each of you. Thank you for loving me while I struggle to figure out how to be the best daddy I can be for you.

Bryan, Rosanne, Scott, Laura, Jeremiah, Jason - thank you all for your support. Having you in my corner means the world. You are always there for advice and constructive feedback. I couldn't ask for better family members or a better support network. I love you all.

Braden. You already got a chunk of a chapter, but you are deserving of so much more. I love you, brother. Thank you for being my best friend and putting up with all that I am. I am not a fun or easy friend to have, yet you have stuck with me through thick and thin and have always been there for me. You have never let me let myself down, and for that, I am eternally grateful.

Julia. Thank you for being my biggest cheerleader and fan! I know that I can always turn to you for a pick me up of honest encouragement. Your feedback and direction helped me maintain my confidence through some dark chapters. I can't thank you enough.

Jim and Christy. Thank you for supporting our family the way that you do. I wouldn't, in good conscious, be able to work on my projects without your support, both of me and my family. Ashley, our girls, and I are all blessed to have you in our lives.

Thank you all for believing in me. In my dark times where I lack trust in myself, you all trust in me to pull through. When I can't lean on myself, I have you all to lean on. For that, I am beyond grateful. I love you all.

/AW/

# INDEX

1. Andersson MA, Conley CS. Optimizing the perceived benefits and health outcomes of writing about traumatic life events. Stress Health. 2013 Feb;29(1):40-9. doi: 10.1002/smi.2423. Epub 2012 Mar 9. PMID: 22407959.

2. Mischkowski, D., et al., Flies on the wall are less aggressive: Self-distancing "in the heat of the moment" reduces aggressive thoughts, angry feelings and aggressive behavior, Journal of Experimental Social Psychology (2012), doi:10.1016/j.jesp.2012.03.012.

3. Kross E, Bruehlman-Senecal E, Park J, Burson A, Dougherty A, Shablack H, Bremner R, Moser J, Ayduk O. Self-talk as a regulatory mechanism: how you do it matters. J Pers Soc Psychol. 2014 Feb;106(2):304-24. doi: 10.1037/a0035173. PMID: 24467424.

4. Daidōji, Y., Cleary, T. F., & Ratti, O. (1999). Code of the samurai: a modern translation of the Bushidō shoshinshū. Boston, Tuttle Pub.

5. Fletcher, D., & Sarkar, M. (2012). A grounded theory of psychological resilience in Olympic champions. *Psychology of Sport and Exercise, 13*(5), 669–678. https://doi.org/10.1016/j.psychsport.2012.04.007

6. Hershfield HE. Future self-continuity: how conceptions of the future self transform intertemporal choice. Ann N Y Acad Sci. 2011 Oct;1235:30-43. doi: 10.1111/j.1749-6632.2011.06201.x. PMID: 22023566; PMCID: PMC3764505.

7. Lyubomirsky, S., Sheldon, K. M., & Schkade, D. (2005). Pursuing Happiness: The Architecture of Sustainable Change. Review of General Psychology, 9(2), 111–131. https://doi.org/10.1037/1089-2680.9.2.111

8. Gelb, M. (2000). How to think like Leonardo Da Vinci: seven steps to genius every day. New York, N.Y., Dell Pub.

9. Bayles, D., & Orland, T. (1993). Art & fear: observations on the perils (and rewards) of artmaking. Santa Cruz, CA : Saint Paul, MN, Image Continuum Press.

10. Evans DR, Boggero IA, Segerstrom SC. The Nature of Self-Regulatory Fatigue and "Ego Depletion": Lessons From Physical Fatigue. Pers Soc Psychol Rev. 2016 Nov;20(4):291-310. doi: 10.1177/1088868315597841. Epub 2016 Jun 21. PMID: 26228914; PMCID: PMC4788579.

11. Johnston BC, Kanters S, Bandayrel K, Wu P, Naji F, Siemieniuk RA, Ball GD, Busse JW, Thorlund K, Guyatt G, Jansen JP, Mills EJ. Comparison of weight loss among named diet programs in overweight and obese adults: a meta-analysis. JAMA. 2014 Sep 3;312(9):923-33. doi: 10.1001/jama.2014.10397. PMID: 25182101.

12. Singh B, Olds T, Curtis R, *et al*Effectiveness of physical activity interventions for improving depression, anxiety and distress: an overview of systematic reviews*British Journal of Sports Medicine* Published Online First: 16 February 2023. doi: 10.1136/bjsports-2022-106195

13. Dweck, C. S. (2008). *Mindset: the new psychology of success.* Ballantine Books trade pbk. ed. New York, Ballantine Books.

14. Becker-Phelps,L. Ph.D. (2013, October 14) Accept Your Pain; It Will Hurt Less. Accepting reality leads to change like denial never can. https://www.psychologytoday.com/us/blog/making-change/201310/accept-your-pain-it-will-hurt-less

15. Stallard, William, "A Resilient Warrior: Coping Positively With Combat Stress Exposure" (2014). *Walden Dissertations and Doctoral Studies*. 1768. https://scholarworks.waldenu.edu/dissertations/1768

16. Beckwith, M. B. (2008). *Life visioning.* Unabridged. [United States], Sounds True.